The Language of Journalism

A multi-genre perspective

**ANGELA SMITH AND
MICHAEL HIGGINS**

BLOOMSBURY

LONDON • NEW DELHI • NEW YORK • SYDNEY

Bloomsbury Academic

An imprint of Bloomsbury Publishing Plc

1385 Broadway	50 Bedford Square
New York	London
NY 10018	WC1B 3DP
USA	UK

www.bloomsbury.com

First published 2013

Library of Congress Cataloging-in-Publication Data
Higgins, Michael, 1967-
The language of journalism : a multi-genre perspective / by Michael Higgins and
Angela Smith.
pages cm
Includes bibliographical references and index.
ISBN 978-1-84966-066-2 (pbk. : alk. paper) 1. Journalism–Language.
I. Smith, Angela (College teacher) II. Title.
PN4771.H54 2013
070.4'014–dc23
2012051335

ISBN: PB: 978-1-8496-6066-2
e-pdf: 978-1-7809-3228-6
e-pub: 978-1-7809-3227-9

Typeset by Newgen Imaging Systems Pvt Ltd, Chennai, India
Printed and bound in Great Britain

Contents

List of figures

Acknowledgements

We are indebted to the people who have supported and encouraged the research that has gone into this book over the past few years. In particular, to the students who have taken the 'Introduction to Media Language' module at the University of Sunderland, and to the various people who have taught this module over the years, particularly Mary Talbot, who devised the early version of this module, Michael Pearce and John-Paul Stephenson. We would also like to acknowledge the invaluable suggestions made by colleagues in the Ross Priory Broadcast Talk seminar group, whose comments and encouragement have helped us a great deal.

Thanks also to Emily Dodd at Bloomsbury, who originally commissioned this book, and to Katie Gallof for her limitless patience and good humour.

Most of all, both authors are grateful for the love and forbearance of their respective parents.

1

Introduction: Why should we study the language of journalism?

Journalism serves as the very oxygen of public life. Most of what we know about issues from the goings-on in neighbouring countries, to the state of Royal marriages, to the taxes we are likely to pay, we get from media reports. Not only is journalism 'organised gossip', as Edward Egglestone is reported to have said, but it also provides us with much of the raw material we draw upon to gossip among ourselves. Since journalism is so firmly a part of the social firmament, it is not surprising that almost everyone feels able to offer normative assessments of journalistic performance, with their own instincts on what characterizes good and bad examples of the craft. However, in order to discuss journalism in a systematic, genuinely informed and evidence-based way – comparing journalistic texts with one another, thinking about the history and practices of the profession, assessing its contemporary state – we need to have a set of tools. It is these tools this book hopes to provide.

Any examination of journalism is likely to be interested in *what* journalism covers. The items that make up the news agenda are not randomly assembled, nor are they the outcome of a natural and unchanging order. Rather, journalism is a matter of selection. Moreover, this is informed selection on the part of journalists themselves and the institutions for which they work. The procedures of selection draw upon particular criteria, which we will discuss later in the book as 'news values'. Knowledge on our part of these news values and their limits provide a framework for understanding why some things are thought of as having 'news' potential while most things are not. The craft of journalism is not just finding stories that meet the criteria for news, but being able to construct an account of these events that give prominence to their most newsworthy characteristics.

This leads us to the *language* of journalism. The analysis of journalism's language allows us to look at *how* journalism builds stories, how these stories function as arguments, and how the linguistic construction of the story shapes the way in which it is to be understood. But the role of language is more complex that providing the component parts. Language is, after all, the most essential tool of the journalist, and it is one of the marks of the exceptional journalist that they are able to use language with creativity and style. Along with the professional practices of investigation, interviewing and fact-checking, the accomplished journalist knows that it is the ability to work with language and manipulate its emotive thrust that gives the story its shape and resonance. Without language, journalism would be no more than a picture book or a silent film. This is why it is important for us to study the language used.

To begin with, we will look at five interrelated ways in which language operates, and which emphasizes its place at the centre of our understanding of journalism.

Language is social

Language is what makes us human. From our earliest months of life, we strive to communicate with the world around us through language and try to develop new skills and an expanded vocabulary in order to do this. This means that the language we acquire is one that is associated with our immediate community. As Paul Gee (1999: 82) explains, language simultaneously reflects reality ('the way things are') and constructs it to be a certain way. In this way, language is dynamic and constantly changing to reflect changing social contexts and our need to communicate within these. We expand our repertoire of linguistic styles and registers as our experiences of our social worlds increase. Accordingly, despite a considerable degree of linguistic competence, the pre-school child has limited communication skills compared with those of the average university student. The language we use in the pub when talking to friends is very different from that we would use when giving a presentation in class to that same group of friends. We have sufficient linguistic competency to realize that there are different requirements placed upon us in different social contexts.

Because these competencies are rarely explicitly taught to us and yet are common conventions, we can say that we have assumptions and attitudes about language use which will reflect our attitudes about language users. This can be at a basic level of accent and dialect – in British national TV news it is still unusual for the main news presenter to have a regional English accent that is not closely associated with Received Pronunciation (RP) (particular dispensation appears to be given to the Scots, Welsh or Irish accents of the home nations). Indeed, such is the stigma associated with certain regional accents of England, even in the twenty-first century, that mainstream news broadcasters shy away from regionally identified accents, preferring the region-neutral but socially specific RP (Smith, 2009; Crystal, 2010).

The background knowledge of the reader or listener is also called upon to create a sense of common social identity, such that journalism fosters community by drawing upon a linguistic repertoire in common with the audience. This is never more apparent than when the arrangement breaks down. An example of such a collapse in understanding occurred on the BBC Radio 4 flagship news programme *Today* during a heated exchange between the long-time presenter James Naughtie and the then–business secretary Peter Mandleson (3 December 2009). Naughtie drew on his personal social world to emphasize his frustration in failing to get a 'straight' answer from Mandleson by saying it was 'rather like talking to Poo-Bah'.[1] Mandleson immediately pleaded unfamiliarity with the reference, requiring the interviewer to place his questioning to one side in order to employ twin strategies of repair and explanation. In the shamble of apology and clarification that followed, the main point of Naughtie's challenge was lost. This serves as an important illustration of how the pertinence of an argument's rhetoric, and therefore its overall coherence, depends on the journalist and the listener (and in this case, interviewee) inhabiting a world of shared background knowledge.

Language enacts identity and the right to speak

The next factor that we need to understand is that language apportions a particular identity to the person writing or speaking. Often, this is unrelated to the original source of the text. Even when the person who writes a script may not be the person who delivers it, it is the one delivering the script that is responsible for it. We see this happening on a daily basis in politics, where speechwriters are often anonymous but their words can have far-reaching effects with the speaker being held accountable for what they say. John Searle (1969: 54) describes these demands as the 'felicity conditions' that we attach to utterances. Not only should something be true, but the person that is speaking should have the right to say it. This enactment of identity means we come to anticipate certain people performing certain linguistic acts, as well as being responsible for commenting on given events in their capacity as the appropriate social actor. Just as a priest is professionally entitled to declare a marriage if the appropriate conditions are met, so is a journalist entitled to express public outrage.

Through the examples to come we will find that our consideration of the appropriateness of utterances should be thought about alongside the management of personality and professional reputation among journalists. A well-known social actor in one field shifting to another, such as from politics to humour, attracts attention. In Britain, for example, the well-known broadcast journalist Jeremy Paxman, usually associated with 'serious' news as the presenter of BBC2's *Newsnight* programme, attracted widespread media attention and derision when he stepped out of his 'serious news' role and made public comments about the quality of men's underwear. This expedition into the trivial led to several newspapers punning on Paxman as 'Pantsman'. Different judgements of appropriateness were applied to war correspondent Kate Adie's decision to cover a domestic tragedy in the Scottish town of Dunblane (Smith and Higgins, 2012). The analysis of journalism is bound up with appropriateness, expectation and professional practice, often bound in personal or institutional personalities – licence to court public outrage on some issues, and a professional bar on wandering into others.

Journalistic language denotes agency and power

Just as we began by telling you that journalism is important, you can be equally assured that the vitality of journalism forms part of its very expression. In large part, this is offered as power on behalf of the readers or listeners, where language is used to imply a degree of interactivity between journalists and individual readers. Sometimes this can be through exposing wrongdoing or arguing for or against something, whereby the dynamic verb choices are often associated with such leaders as 'The *Sun* says . . .' and 'Have your say', even 'Sign our online petition'. In this way, journalists imply there is a social influence to their profession and they pursue their responsibilities diligently.

However, the distribution of this power is hierarchical and dependent upon the needs of the story, and the opinions of certain people can be considered more creditable and authoritative than those of others, depending on the circumstances (Montgomery, 2007). For example, in anti-war stories, news journalism is more likely to feature the voices of mothers of service personnel who have died in Iraq or Afghanistan than the voices of anti-war campaigners who have less personal involvement in the conflict. These experiential voices carry more emotional weight for audiences and can be treated as expert opinions. Expert opinion in other contexts might come from the voices of scientists whose opinions are sought on topics such as climate change. When the interview moves to global policies to deal with climate change, then accountability interviewees may be called in, people such as politicians and business leaders who can be held institutionally accountable for dealing with such policies. Journalism is thereby implicated in both the distribution and the exercise of power, and uses language strategically in discharging both of these.

We will find that power and identity are important components in the language of journalism. As Maxwell McCombs (2004) famously notes, journalism has the potential to influence the ways in which people think by setting the agendas of public discussion. News can reinforce people's beliefs about such issues as immigration, which is widely regarded in the right-wing British press as being wholly negative. It can shape opinions, such as attitudes towards political parties. Britain's best-selling red-top tabloid newspaper, the *Sun*, famously declared 'It's the *Sun* wot won it' after backing Tony Blair's New Labour party prior to victory in the 1997 general election. To give a brief example of the implication of language in this, the *Sun*'s style of headline writing employs non-standard English which reflects and reaches out to the working-class social identity of its perceived readers.

Language is political

Language, thus, can be used to persuade, argue, inform, expose: it is never altogether neutral. Journalism expresses and speaks to communities of understanding, and so its language always contains layers of meaning that go beyond mere points of view. As we will see in the course of this book, journalism can only ever strive to be neutral or objective, and linguistic analysis can help to uncover the strategies and pitfalls of this endeavour. For example, we will look at how certain linguistic choices of word or phrase or grammatical structure can reveal points of view. Sometimes this is clear, such as in the reporting of the Iraq War, where initially this was referred to as the 'US *liberation* of Iraq', however 'victory' was less than conclusive and thus that conflict came to be referred to as the 'US-led *invasion* of Iraq'. Elsewhere, news reporting of the 2008 Israeli/Palestinian conflict was articulated as Israel invading Gaza, or as Israel defending its borders. Or to take another example, the insidious demonization of young people leads to stories of party-goers being rearticulated as 'drunken teenagers' or more specifically in the case of women, 'ladettes', who are the subjects of moral panic over the perceived decline in moral standards among young women.

Language is an instrument that is shaped according to material circumstances and the purposes it needs to serve. Language is a medium of power and can be used to legitimate inequalities and unjust social relations for political ends. It can thus be used to empower as well as disempower. Commonplace public discussion can often centre on whether a story is biased in some way, but it is through linguistic analysis that we can uncover just how this comes to be.

How to analyse language

In this book, we will be using Critical Discourse Analysis (CDA) as the main analytical model. This has developed as an area of linguistic analysis under such theorists as Kress (1985), Fairclough (1989) and Fowler et al. (1979) to explore areas of social activity and the complex relationships between language and social practice. This approach to research affords a more dialectic view that allows for the investigation of language as reflecting and also shaping and maintaining social realities. As developed by Fairclough, CDA is heavily influenced by Marxism; in particular, the impact of Foucault's work on power and discourse is significant. CDA's explicitly political agenda seeks to raise awareness of the ideological frameworks that inform language choice, and the construction, representation and positioning of its subjects in discourse. This will be discussed in more detail below.

Discourse, ideology, power

The definition of discourse is open to several different views. In the area of conversation analysis, 'discourse' can be used to refer to spoken interaction. In this usage, we 'discourse', that is, speak. In CDA, the use of discourse is modelled on Foucault's usage of it in cultural studies, but not defined by him. In this sense, discourse refers not only to language but also to sets of social and cultural practices. In the early development of CDA, Fairclough and Wodak (1997: 258) argued: '[D]iscourse is socially constitutive as well as socially conditioned – it constitutes situations, objects of knowledge, and the social identities of and relationships between people and groups of people. It is constitutive both in the sense that it helps to sustain and reproduce the social status quo, and in the sense that it contributes to transforming it.' This argument shows that there are important issues of power involved as a social consequence, and this in turn may have major ideological effects in that discourses 'can help produce and reproduce unequal power relations between (for instance) social classes, women and men, and ethnic/cultural majorities and minorities through the ways in which they represent things and position people' (ibid.). This definition broadly encompasses the analysis of textual form, structure and organization from the level of phonology to generic structure. Within linguistics, different approaches have tended to focus on specific levels. For example, in French discourse analysis, the focus is on lexical semantics, while in critical linguistics the focus is on grammar and lexis. However, Riesigl and Wodak point out:

> Whether analysts with a critical approach prefer to focus on microlinguistic features, macrolinguistic features, textual, discursive or contextual features, whether their angle is primarily philosophical, sociological or historical – in most studies there is reference to Hallidayan systemic functional grammar. (2001: 8)

Texts function within 'discourses'. We should think about discourses within the Foucauldian tradition: they are historically constituted bodies of knowledge and practices that shape people, giving positions of power to some but not to others.

Ideology

The term 'ideology' has been used in many different ways by social theorists, largely owing to the way in which ideology has been applied to answer very different questions. Although the concept of 'ideology' precedes Marxism itself, it is an important concept in almost all Marxist thinking about culture.

According to John Frow (1989: 207), Foucault argued against 'the normativeness of any conception of ideology', choosing to focus instead on a description of the determinations according to which discourses have historically been distributed between the true and false. While rejecting the notion of ideology in his earlier works, Foucault does not see power as functioning as a unidirectional chain of effects, rather seeing it as 'deployed and exercised through a net-like organisation' (Foucault, 1981: 98). While Foucault sought to demonstrate that those in a position of hierarchical power, such as the lawmakers and the sovereign, may have positions of dominance, he directs our attention 'away from the grand, overall strategies of power, towards the many, localised circuits, tactics, mechanisms and effects through which power circulates' (Hall, 1997: 50), particularly in our case through the media.

However, Macdonald (2003: 36) insists that Foucault's model is attempting to 'sideline ideology', and 'reduces the possibility of distinguishing between different types of power. The charge of relativism, or treating as equal operations of power that are very different in their consequences, seems difficult to refute'. We would agree with Macdonald that, while Foucault's work on discourse is useful for the insight it provides on the operation of power through symbolic forms, the term 'ideology' still has currency when evaluating relations of power. It is still necessary to remain attentive to those regimes of influence that centralize power and employ it in relations of dominance.

This requires a broad and inclusive definition of ideology. Broadening the concept of ideology from its Marxist inception, as Terry Eagleton comments, moves us away from conceptualizing ideology simply as ruling belief systems that seek to preserve the status quo but to refer to 'any kind of intersection between belief systems and political power [. . .] whether this intersection challenged or confirmed a particular social order' (1991: 6).

For the purposes of this book, we will take it to mean a 'set of beliefs or values that can be explained through the (non-cognitive) interest or position of some social group' (Elster, 1982: 123). In this way ideology is structured discourse, and is directly or indirectly based on or generated by a set of mutually interdependent categories. As adopted by Eagleton and Macdonald, this reformulation of ideology does not deny how ideology operates through 'such devices as unification, spurious identification, deception, self-deception, universalisation and rationalisation' (Eagleton, 1991: 222). Antoni Gramsci's notion of hegemony is useful to theorize how ideology works in this way.

Gramsci claimed that dominant groups rule by consent and that 'in order to win consent, the dominant group cannot count on the power and material force which such a position gives in order to exercise political leadership' (1998: 210) but must rely on a 'multitude of other so-called private initiatives and activities which form the apparatus of the political and cultural hegemony of the working classes' (215). The dominant ideologies are not imposed on our consciousness, but rather they dovetail into ways of thinking that seem to make sense, or even be viewed as being common sense. Such a model 'captures the effectiveness of forms of appeal that speak to our senses of expediency while masking their tendentiousness' (ibid), and recognizes that ideology is only ever encountered in what Bennett (1998) refers to as a 'compromised form': one which is not static but forever shifting through the constant negotiation and contestation of differing and changing social and political circumstances. A nuanced approach therefore acknowledges the agency of social subjects to make choices, albeit limited, depending on their cultural positioning instead of being reduced to becoming merely the effects and vehicles of power.

Texts and social structures

Texts can be very useful to assist in developing an understanding of how discourses, ideology and power operate in society. As Fairclough has commented, they can be seen as 'sensitive barometers of social processes, movement and diversity, and textual analysis can provide particularly good indicators of social change' (Jaworski and Coupland, 1999: 204). They provide evidence of these ongoing processes, and thus offer a rich source of data for research. In this book, we draw on a variety of media texts which include print, broadcast and digital platforms. A much-criticized aspect of Foucault's hugely influential work on discourse is that he failed to provide specific and detailed evidence of texts to support his historical studies of discourse. In spite of this, the specifically linguistic analysis of texts provides support to Foucault's underlying genealogical methodology for analysis. Jürgen Habermas claims that 'language is also a medium of domination and social force. It serves to legitimise relations of organised power. In so far as the legitimations of power relations, [. . .] are not articulated, [. . .] language is also ideological' (1987: 259). This is a claim that would probably be endorsed by most critical discourse analysts. Commenting on the usefulness of textual analysis in this area, Fairclough states:

> It is increasingly through texts [. . .] that social control and social domination are exercised (and indeed negotiated and resisted). Textual analysis, as a part of critical discourse analysis, can therefore be an important political resource. (Jaworski and Coupland, 1999: 205)

As Wodak (2002) explains, a fully 'critical' account of discourse requires a theorization and description of both the social processes and structures which leads to the production of a text, and of the social structures and processes within which individuals or groups as social historical subjects create meanings in their interaction with texts. Consequently, three concepts feature in CDA: the concept of power, the concept of history and the concept of ideology. If we accept that discourse is structured by dominance, then the history of a given discourse is tied up with the history and development of those systems of dominance. In other words, it is situated in time and space, and the dominant structures are legitimated by ideologies of powerful groups. CDA makes it possible to analyse pressures from above and possibilities of resistance to unequal power relationships that are made to appear as societal conventions. According to this view, dominant structures stabilize conventions and naturalize them. Explicitly, the effects of power and ideology in the production of meaning are obscured and acquire stable and natural forms: they are taken as 'given'. Resistance is then seen as the breaking of conventions, of stable discursive practices, in what Fairclough (1993) refers to as acts of 'creativity'.

To the extent that much of social science shares a concern with the relationship between text, practice and relations of dominance, CDA provides a generally useful resource. As we will see throughout this book, different journalistic products produce 'common sense' discourses such as the examples briefly discussed above (Israel 'invading Gaza' or 'defending its borders').

The development of CDA

Critical Discourse Analysis grew out of the work of British and Australian pioneers of Critical Linguistics, particularly Fowler and Kress, in convergence with the approaches of British discourse analyst Norman Fairclough and the Dutch text linguist Teun van Dijk. CDA has produced the majority of the research into media discourse during the 1980s and 1990s, and 'has arguably become the standard framework for studying media texts within European linguistics and discourse studies' (Bell and Garrett, 1998: 6).

In the tradition of critical theory, CDA aims to make transparent the discursive aspects of societal disparities and inequalities. CDA in the majority of cases takes the part of the underprivileged and tries to expose the linguistic means used by the privileged to stabilize or even to intensify inequalities in society. Most frequently, CDA has an explicit socio-political agenda, a concern to discover and testify to unequal relations of power which underlie ways of using language in a society, and in particular to reveal the role of discourse in reproducing or challenging socio-political dominance. It also offers the potential for applying theoretically sophisticated frameworks to important issues, so is regarded as being a particularly useful tool for researchers who wish to make their investigation socially active. Work in Australia in the 1990s, initially in the field of educational linguistics, has led to what Martin terms 'Positive Discourse Analysis' (Wodak and Martin, 2003: 4) 'to characterise ideologically orientated research and intervention that examines positive developments with which to make the world a "better" place, and draws on these to intervene in related sites – as a mode of inquiry complementing CDA's focus on language in the service of abusive power' (ibid). This continuity of explicit political intent underpins the approach's on-going concern with theory/practice dialectic. One of the strengths of CDA is that it bases concerns with power and ideology on the detailed linguistic analysis of texts.

Helmer (1993) makes the argument that storytelling too can operate ideologically by 'creating and sustaining symbolic oppositions that enable members to position themselves and others in the organisation', and as such narrative 'serves to strategy the organisation along lines of power, authority, gender and ethics' (34). In relation to gender, Helmer makes the point that women are forced to 'play the patriarchal game' in order to gain some form of economic and political advantage when they are disadvantaged both politically and economically. So, for example, a female actor may turn up at a 'red carpet' event in a revealing outfit, knowing that this will attract media attention. At the UK premier of the 2009 film *Nine*, Nicole Kidman's short shirt in an otherwise demure outfit attracted a great deal of media comment, while her co-star Daniel Day-Lewis's extravagantly high-wasted striped trousers and embroidered shirt passed without comment (*Daily Mail* 4 December 2009). British former glamour model Katie Price attempted to reclaim public sympathy after a messy divorce by claiming sexual abuse by her former husband. In Price's case, this plea for sympathy was only partially successful as more dominant stories of her drunken nights out appeared along side media stories which mused on the whereabouts of her young children. In both cases, discourses that prioritize a conservative performance of femininity are drawn upon to criticize the women concerned.

The model that Fairclough developed for CDA is useful for researchers who share his concerns with language, discourse and power in society. Fairclough's (1995b) model has three components:

1 The first dimension is *text or discourse*, which includes micro texts (e.g. vocabulary, syntax) and macro levels of text structure as well as interpersonal elements in a text.

2 The second is analysis of *discourse practices*. This looks at how a text is constructed and interpreted, and also how it is distributed. Analysis of discourse also considers the discourse practices of different social domains (such as political discourse). Fairclough calls these 'orders of discourse'.

3 The third is analysis of *social practices*, focusing in particular on the relation of discourse to power and ideology.

More simply, this is a method of situating language in its social context (Fairclough's first and third dimensions), looking at the producer/consumer interaction (the second dimension). This is something we will come back to repeatedly in the course of subsequent chapters. For example, we will see how magazine language can be best understood by exploring the social world it is produced in, and for whom in this world it is directed. So we will use CDA to explore how a women's magazine produced in the twenty-first century has concerns with post-feminism and environmentalism, and is underpinned by commercial factors that are widespread in contemporary Western society.

One criticism of CDA has been that the definition of a text is so narrow in that it would not reveal the wider social and discursive practices to be found in other objects for study. However, as Fairclough acknowledges, the wide-ranging cultural studies definition of text 'can obscure important distinctions between different types of cultural artefact, and make the concept of a text rather nebulous by extending it too far' (1995b: 4). Nevertheless, as

Fairclough goes on to say and to explore in more detail in his subsequent work, the broader definition of text is useful in contemporary society as 'texts whose primary semiotic form is language increasingly [have] combined language with other semiotic forms' (1995a: 6). Yet even this has several dimensions of meaning. Written texts can be multi-semiotic, for example, in the typographical design and inclusion of graphics. Other semiotic forms are co-present within a primarily linguistic artefact and interact to produce multi-semiotic texts.

What emerges is a multifunctional idea that texts can be viewed as social spaces in which two fundamental social processes occur at the same time. This involves the analysis of 'the cognition and representation of the world, and social interaction' (Fairclough, 1995a: 6). As Fairclough points out:

> Texts in their ideational functioning constitute systems of knowledge and belief (including what Foucault refers to as 'objects'), and in their interpersonal functioning they constitute social subjects [. . .] and social relations between (categories of) subjects. (1995a: 6)

So this view of texts helps to bring about a practical demonstration of Foucault's (1981) claim about the socially constitutive properties of discourse and text.

Media texts can be categorized under several different genres. As Fairclough argued, a 'genre' may be characterized as the conventionalized, more or less schematically fixed, use of language associated with a particular activity, as a 'socially ratified way of using language in connection with a particular type of social activity' (Fairclough, 1995a: 14). However, Threadgold observes that genres can be more flexible, unpredictable and heterogeneous (Threadgold, 1989). For example, then–prime minister Gordon Brown sent handwritten letters of condolence to the next of kin of those service personnel killed on active service. Dozens of such personal letters were sent during his premiership, but one became a very public document when he was accused of mis-spelling the soldier's family name and the infuriated recipient sent it to a national newspaper (November 2009). Thus the media's appropriation of this text shifted it from a private letter to a public document, and the original message of condolence was lost in the subsequent criticism of Brown's handwriting.

Foucault's concept of 'orders of discourse' (1985) differs in its use by different CDA practitioners. It is taken by Fairclough to 'refer to the ordered set of discursive practices associated with a particular social domain or institution [. . .] and boundaries and relationships between them' (1995a: 12). In general terms, orders of discourse are the ways in which power relationships are enacted, where one participant is positioned in a more powerful position than the other. The more powerful participant evokes this hierarchy of power through language choices, for example, through choosing to accept or reject a contribution or through evoking certain discourses. This is what happened in the case of the letter Gordon Brown sent. Certain sections of the media seized upon it to launch a personal attack on the then–prime minister during a deeply unpopular war rather than assuming an attitude of sympathy towards Brown's visual disability that led to his poor handwriting. In this case, a discourse of national identity took priority over one that dealt in compassion. The boundaries of such discourses are not clearly defined in many cases, and are constantly shifting, reflecting orders of discourse as mediation between the linguistic and the social. Fairclough (1995a) regards changes in the order of social discourse as being in themselves a part of wider processes of socio-cultural change. Official, expert knowledge serves as a means of building up structures of 'truth' or 'normalisation', regulating what can be said and what cannot be. Such debates more recently include those surrounding climate change, wherein the voices of those who oppose policies to limit climate change (such as reducing logging in the Brazilian rain forests) have been largely removed from the debate as presented by the media. Instead, we hear the voices of scientists who live thousands of miles away from the rain forests, but whose contribution is prioritized. Populations can be carefully controlled through the associated disciplinary structures, where certain discursive practices are legitimized and others (usually those of the least powerful) are delegitimized. As Threadgold puts it, such 'expert knowledges thus discursively produce the objects of which they speak and simultaneously exclude those categories which cannot be accounted for within the established "truth"' (1997: 137). As we will see in the more detailed studies that follow in this book, the differently positioned writers and readers across a range of texts that have been produced drawing on differing knowledges and discursive practices will allow for an exploration of aspects of identity and culture.

Drawing on Foucault's earlier work on discourse, Fairclough argues for the place of CDA, suggesting that it

ought in contemporary circumstances to focus its attention upon discourse within the history of the present – changing discursive practices as part of wider processes of social and cultural change – because constant and often dramatic change affecting many domains of social life is a fundamental characteristic of contemporary social experience, because these changes are often constituted to a significant degree by and through changes in discursive practices, and because no proper understanding of contemporary discursive practices is possible that does not attend to that matrix of change. (1995: 19)

Orders of discourse are thus viewed as domains of hegemony and hegemonic struggle. This may be within institutions such as education as well as within the wider social formation. In this process, the ideological investments of particular discursive practices may change.

Many of the journalistic texts we will look at are spoken interactions between two or more participants. This means reference to conversational analysis will be relevant to our exploration of language. John B Thompson (1995) and Martin Montgomery (2007) have explored how spoken interaction can operate in the media. There has been a lot of research in the field of conversation analysis (Hutchby, 2006), and many of the features of such naturally occurring talk are relevant to our study of how language operates in the media. For example, if we accept that the basic expectation of a question is that it requires an answer, then we anticipate there being more than one participant. This links with the principal of turn-taking in conversation, which is one of the basic rules Sacks (1992) listed as components of such interaction. Other features include: in turn-taking where one person talks simultaneously with another, then this is for only a brief time and one participant will 'yield the conversational floor'. Later in this book, we will explore in more detail how this relates to broadcast media texts.

Linked to conversation analysis is Fairclough's work on conversationalization and synthetic personalization (1989). This can be found in various forms of public sphere texts in the late twentieth century and is relevant to our study of media texts. This, as we will see, is closely aligned with informal, spoken language and could be said to be part of the tabloidization of the media (Smith 2009). In Fairclough's definition of synthetic personalization (2001), a media text's producer – whether it is spoken or written – uses linguistic strategies that attempt to present a personal dialogue between individuals. This is achieved through drawing on strategies such as employing personal pronouns (e.g. 'Tell *us* what *you* think'), dialectal features that are presumed to be used by the intended audience/consumer of the text (e.g. '*Stuff* for *blokes*' appearing in a heading for gift ideas in a magazine aimed at young men) and drawing on supposed common knowledge. Grammatically, the use of the question format implies a direct interaction between text producer and reader/listener. For example, the commonly used advertising slogan 'Have you got yours yet?' anticipates the prospective consumer will respond and rush out to acquire the advertised goods or service.

As Wodak (2002: 11) comments, an important perspective in CDA is that it is very rare for a text to be the work of any one person. In texts discursive differences are negotiated; they are governed by differences in power which are themselves in part encoded in and determined by discourse and by genre. Texts are often sites of struggle, showing traces of differing discourses and ideologies contending with the dominant power.

It is not only the notion of struggles for power and control but also the intertextuality and recontextualization of competing discourses that can be revealed by CDA.

The three-dimensional framework for CDA as outlined by Fairclough includes the analysis of discursive practices. This relates to the processes of a text's production, distribution and consumption, and ensures that a text is not isolated from the institutional and discursive practices within which it is embedded. Within the scope of our analysis of media texts, the text can be reviewed with reference to the diverse ways in which it could be interpreted and responded to. This approach to text analysis owes much to Morley's work on audience reception in media studies (1980), extending this from examining the moment of reception to consideration of how texts are taken up and transformed in various spheres of life (such as family, work, leisure activities, etc.).

In this model of CDA, the Gramscian theory of hegemony (in analysis of socio-cultural practice) is combined with the Bakhtinian theory of genre (in analysis of discourse practice – defining genre as discourses, narratives, registers, etc.). Bakhtin's work on text and genre (Jaworski and Coupland, 1999) argues for the inclusion of intertextual analysis as a necessary complement to linguistic analysis in the studying of texts, as such an approach draws attention to the dependence of text on society and history in the form of the resources made available within the order of discourse. According to Bakhtin (1986: 65), genres 'are the drive belts from the history of society to the history of language'. This dynamic conception of intertextual analysis highlights how texts can transform social and historical resources, and how genres can be mixed within a text.

Intertextuality

The term 'intertextuality' was devised by Kristeva in relation to Bakhtin's discussion of the transposition of sign systems of carnival, courtly poetry and scholastic discourse into the novel (Threadgold 1997: 66). Her use of this term closely follows that of Foucault, although Foucault himself did not use this label, instead describing how statements can only exist in connection with other statements (1981: 98). At its most fundamental level, as Bakhtin observes, intertextuality is inherent in language as part of its comprehensibility. The speaker

> is not, after all, the first speaker, the one who disturbs the eternal silence of the universe. And he [sic] presupposes not only the existence of the language system he is using, but also the existence of preceding utterances – his own and others' – with which his given utterance enters

into one kind of relation or another (builds on them, polemicizes with them, or simply presumes that they are already known to the listener). (1986: 124)

Bakhtin's writings on text and genre (1986) argue for intertextual analysis as a necessary component of linguistic analysis, an argument that has been taken up by Kress and Threadgold (1989), Thibault (1991), Talbot (1995) and Fairclough (1992, 1995a, 2003). The use of the concept of intertextuality in linguistics has been particularly important in relation to the development of CDA. In this model, as Threadgold states, '[t]exts are now understood to be constructed chunk by chunk, intertextually, not word by word, and there can thus be no link between text and context except through the intertextual resources of this discursively produced subjectivity' (1997: 3).

Fairclough expands on this, arguing that intertextuality is used to draw attention to the dependence of texts upon societal and historical discursive formations in the form of the resources made available within the order of discourse (Fairclough, 1995a: 188). The concept of cultural capital, as explored by Bourdieu (1991), is relevant here as access to the range of texts from which interpretation may be drawn is not equally distributed. We saw an example of this earlier in James Naughtie's exchange with Peter Mandleson. Culler (1975) and Barthes (1970/1975) expand intertextuality to include the reader as a constituent component. Culler described intertextuality as the general discursive space in which meaning is made possible and intelligible (1981: 103). Thus, for Fairclough:

Discourses and texts which occur within them have histories, they belong to historical series, and the interpretation of intertextual context is a matter of deciding which series a text belongs to, and therefore what can be taken as common ground for participants, or presupposed. [. . .] Discourse participants may arrive at roughly the same interpretation or different ones, and the interpretation of the more powerful participant may be imposed upon others. (1989: 152)

So the intertextual resources each person has available to them can be limited, leading to a restricted understanding. This link between intertextuality and power makes it an important part of Fairclough's three-part model for CDA. As he argues, 'intertextual analysis crucially mediates the connection between language and social context, and facilitates more satisfactory bridging of the gap between texts and contexts' in his three-part model, whereby intertextual analysis occupies a mediating position (1995a: 198).

Holquist relates Bakhtin's notion of the dialogic nature of intertextuality to power, arguing that 'a word, discourse, language or culture undergoes "dialogization" when it becomes relativized, de-privileged, aware of competing definitions for the same things. Undialogized language is authoritative or absolute' (1981: 427). As Holquist suggests, there is a difference in the degree to which texts may be 'dialogic'. Fairclough (2003: 47) offers a general summary of the effects of the dialogicality:

Most dialogical	Attributes, quotes
	Modalized assertion
	Non-modalized assertion
Least dialogical	Assumption

In this way, we can understand this model as 'less dialogicality' carrying with it consensus, with a 'normalisation and acceptance of differences of power which brackets or suppresses differences in meaning and norms' (Fairclough, 2003: 42).

On other occasions, my data also shows evidence of individuals using state-gathered information for their own means. As Foucault noted:

[P]ower and resistance to power are not conceivable as opposites, statically ranged against each other, but as fluid force relations that group together, temporarily and uneasily, in oppositional formulations [. . .] Where there is power, there is resistance, and yet or rather consequently, this resistance is never in a position of exteriority to power. (1981: 34)

Yet this appearance of resistance is something that we ought not to romanticize, Abu-Lughod has argued, saying that 'we should learn to read in various local and everyday resistance the existence of a range of specific strategies and structures of power' (1990: 53). In identifying and exploring the manifestations of 'resistance', we can see in greater detail the complex workings of power relations.

The use of dialogical elements in a text allows for other 'voices' to be heard, and is at its most dialogicalized in this development of intertextualization. This can be analysed in terms of power relations: Whose 'voice' is allowed by the text's producer? What are they allowed to contribute? How is this being contextualized? This 'editing' process of dialogicalization can be used to exclude as well as include other voices. We will look at this in detail in the chapter exploring magazine features.

Where we go from here:
The structure of the book

Having explained some key components and techniques of language and discourse analysis, the rest of the chapters are divided according to genre and media platform. This spread of media platforms is designed to enable us to look across a diverse range of journalistic forms, and to examine both written and spoken forms of news delivery. We have set out the book so that different chapters develop particular themes, and draw upon varying strategies of analysis. In doing this, we are able to explore how the several angles of analysis we have called upon tease out different discourses. Some of these discourses we will find across more than one chapter, such as the place of gender across both magazines and newspapers and the importance of national identity in both broadcast news and sports journalism. Others, such as sociability in broadcasting, are concentrated within particular chapters. Importantly, this should not be taken to mean that these discourses are contained within given genres. Quite the opposite in fact, as you are invited to think about and explore how various discourses, communicative strategies and forms of commonality might have a role across various forms of journalism. In using this book, you might productively reflect on the place of gender in broadcast news, for example, as well as perhaps whatever strains of national identification sustain through online journalism. We are therefore dedicated to showing you some sense of the diversity not just in the language of journalism and the contexts in which it appears, but also in the dynamism and flexibility in how it has come to be used, and the tools that available to examine it afresh.

Broadcast journalism

We begin by looking at broadcast journalism: the dialogic aspects of journalism as found in interaction between participants who are using spoken language. The features of spoken language we find here has become increasingly informal, something Fairclough refers to as 'conversationalization' of public discourse (see also Smith, 2009). The general features of such spoken language that we will look at in this chapter have fed into printed forms of journalism, as we will see in later chapters. In this chapter, we will explore a variety of journalistic texts from the broadcast media, including television and radio. As well as scripted news, the chapter will examine the interaction between news journalists and studio-based news presenters, and interviews with non-media interactants. The relevance of visual aspects of TV broadcast journalism will also be discussed. Much of the analysis will be informed by issues of balance and bias in individual journalists' broadcast reports, and the implications of liveness and unscripted journalism. The chapter will also examine how language study offers an insight into the processes involved in turning reporters' notes into a broadcast script.

Magazine journalism

After looking at spoken language used in broadcast journalism, we move to the simulation of this in print media. We will find that Fairclough's work on synthetic personalization can be applied to written texts where the strategies of spoken language will be applied in the creation of a friendly, approachable community of readers. This chapter, therefore, will explore the linguistic features and discourses of magazine journalism. It will look at the visual components of magazine journalism, and the influence of advertising on the visual and written forms used in magazines. The chapter will also look at the various genres of magazine, including literary and celebrity magazines, and will examine the implications of these for journalistic writing with particular reference to issues of gender.

Newspaper journalism

We will now move on to the language found in newspaper journalism, seeing how the features of spoken language we have seen in previous chapters are most often found in news headlines. As well as differences between 'quality' and 'popular' newspapers, and those between national cultures, the various genres of newspaper journalism – editorial, opinion, news and feature coverage – will be outlined, and the significance of the linguistic styles employed in each one fully explored.

Sports reporting

In this chapter, we will explore how this variety of journalism is a combination of spoken and written language. In looking at sports reporting, we will focus on the characteristics of sports commentary. Of particular interest to this chapter will be the extent to which sports commentary draws upon and deals with the norms and expectations of other forms of journalism, such as the distinctions between description and comment. The chapter will also be concerned with the management of spontaneity and the consequences of live broadcasting for journalistic form, and the recreation of this in print media.

We will also draw on the way national identity comes into sports reporting, and particularly how this can be used to articulate prejudices that are akin to racism in certain high-profile contexts.

Online journalism

The final chapter will look at more recent developments in journalism. It will look at the online presence of newspapers and broadcasters, examining both the formative constraints and the development of new forms of journalistic language. The chapter will show how multi-modal approaches to discourse are useful in comprehending the relationship between language and other aspects of online provision, and will look at the influence of these emergent forms on institutional news sites as well as other social media platforms such as Facebook, Twitter and YouTube. We will see how the conversational nature of journalistic language is present in this form, in particular as untrained reporters – citizen journalists – increasingly make an important contribution to media reporting.

It will look at the development of a 'structured unconventionality' within amateur and fan journalism, and will reflect on how this has flourished in the online environment. The chapter will also examine the linguistic characteristics associated with news-dedicated weblogs, taking account of such factors as the emphasis on opinion and authorship; conclusions will be offered regarding the implications of these for journalism practice. The chapter will examine the extent to which the practices of citizen-produced journalism are becoming incorporated within conventional journalism institutions, both online and elsewhere.

News values

This introductory chapter will conclude with an introductory summary of news values and their importance. Before we can claim any insight into the language of journalism, it is necessary for us to have a system for reflecting on what it is journalists are trying to do. In a now well-known essay on Norwegian news coverage of international affairs, Johan Galtung and Mari Ruge (1965) proposed a series of 'news values': a list amounting to 12 factors.

1 *Frequency* determines that an event should unfold at a rate appropriate to the given media, be it an hourly radio update or a weekly newspaper.

2 Events are judged according to a *threshold of magnitude*, the larger, or the more violent.

3 News should be *unambiguous*, militating against events that demand a complex or nuanced interpretation.

4 An event should be *culturally meaningful*, to the extent that it should have a particular resonance within the contexts of production and consumption.

5 The event should in *consonance* with what the news organization expects to cover.

6 Yet, news should have an *unexpected* element of novelty and surprise.

7 Also, news is often a *continuation* of an on-going story, as much as once an event becomes a part of the news agenda, further developments on the same story are likely to be covered as well.

8 Further, an event also has to fit with the *compositional requirements* of the news outlet at a given time, where particular genres of story have to be catered to, including politics and sport for example.

9 In addition, references to so-called *elite nations* are of more consequence than places considered more economically and culturally removed.

10 Similarly, *elite people* such as political leaders and celebrities are more consequential than others in news selection.

11 On the other hand, references to 'persons' more generally feed the appetite for *human interest* in news, as well as broader inclinations to empathize with the subjects of a story.

12 Finally, the imperative for *negativity* guides journalists towards unanticipated disasters and scandal, rather than the routine and functional.

Galtung and Ruge's taxonomy is driven by the observation that the great majority of events in the world are not thought of as 'news'. Even occurrences of some significance will be considered newsworthy in some contexts and not in others. Town hall corruption will be newsworthy in that particular town, but perhaps of less interest further afield. Galtung and Ruge suggest these news values as the criteria according to which particular items can be thought of as 'news', while most things are so clearly not. In addition, they suggest that such values also cast light on the hierarchies of importance that obtain between comparatively similar stories: Why do misdeeds in one town hall make the national news, for example, while others are only of local interest? Together, these news values constitute the 'common sense' behind what makes a compelling news story: on some occasions offering an explicit framework for judging one potential story against the next, while more often describing an unconscious set of professional perceptual practices.

There have been several reconfigurations of Galtung and Ruge's original taxonomy. Allan Bell (1991: 156–159), for example, introduces a number of additional factors that will prove useful in looking at how journalism is expressed. He points out that news is defined by 'recency', meaning that journalism routinely places stress on the currency of the account. Linked to this, Bell highlights the 'competition' between different news providers: to be seen to outperform one another in breaking news stories, and depth of detail. Also, Bell emphasizes the influence of 'attribution'; that is, the quality of sources available and whether these correspond with such values of elite persons and human interest as will help in determining news selection. Fourth, and importantly, Bell directs us to the issue of 'facticity': the obligation of news to truthfulness, and in particular the production of 'the kind of facts and figures on which hard news thrives: locations, names, sums of money, numbers of all kinds'. Another of the most notable revisions of news values is that by Tony Harcup and Deirdre O'Neill (2001), who examine the relevance of the list to the contemporary British context. Of the revised list suggested by them, the main differences are an increase in the newsworthiness of 'celebrities', an emphasis on news relating to the entertainment industry, and attention to the political agenda and market position of the news organization itself.

To conclude, therefore, news values are an attempt to render the daily, instinctive decisions of professional journalism tangible. A number of complementary taxonomies are available – Teun van Dijk (1983) offers a slight variation, for example – but the ones we have highlighted are as follows:

- Frequency
- Threshold
- Unambiguous
- Culturally relevant
- Consonance
- Unexpectedness
- Continuation
- Composition
- Elite nations
- Elite people
- Human interest
- Negativity

  (Galtung and Ruge, 1965)

- Recency
- Competition
- Attribution
- Facticity

  (Bell, 1991)

- Celebrity
- Entertainment
- The agenda of the news organization

  (Harcup and O'Neill, 2001)

As we progress through this book, then, the use of critical discourse analysis as outlined here will help us explore how journalistic language articulates these news values in the various genres and modes by which 'news' is spread by the media.

Note

1 Poo-Bah is a character in Gilbert and Sullivan's comic opera *The Mikado*, who exhibits haughty, high self-regard for himself.

2

Broadcast journalism

Introduction

This chapter will explore some of the methods and principles described in Chapter 1 within the fields of broadcast journalism, including examples from both radio and television. Broadcast journalism offers up a peculiar set of practices and opportunities for thinking about the relationship between language and journalism. This should come as no surprise as journalism moves across different media platforms it develops in to take advantage of whatever innovative forms of engagement become possible. As we noted in the introductory chapter, one of the characteristics of both scripted and unscripted broadcast talk is an increase in informality (Montgomery 2007; Smith 2009). In spite of the pronounced asymmetry in power in the status of the journalist against the presumed audience member, and even as the content of the news aspires to accuracy and authority, broadcast journalism increasingly styles itself as unstuffy and relaxed.

Throughout, we should keep in mind that journalism is primarily concerned with the production of news content to agreed professional standards. As the chapter proceeds, we are also therefore going to look at those issues of balance and diligent practice around which broadcast journalism is judged. We will look at how news values are emphasized in the news script as it is broadcast, and reflect on how attention to the conventions of news, both recent and emerging, help us to understand the way language is used in broadcast journalism.

Broadcast and interaction

The imperative of informality in broadcasting also manifests in what appears to be a loosening of the relationship between the broadcaster and the audience. The capacity for engaging in 'para-social interaction' – described by Horton and Wohl (1982: 188) as 'the illusion of face-to-face relationship [between the audience and] the performer' – has become one of the key skills of the broadcast journalist. And as media platforms begin to converge, with digital and online communication streams allowing varying degrees of live audience feedback, this 'conversation with the audience' edges more towards a genuine two-way arrangement, where news producers are able to interact with the audience in real time, involving members of the audience through phone-ins, text messaging, Twitter and emails. This is an arrangement capable of altering the content of the journalism and changing as the broadcast proceeds, in addition to generating ongoing conversation and comment, as well as feedback afterwards.

Because media organizations are rarely required to pay for this extra audience-generated content, it is relatively cheap to introduce. In her 2003 book *Ordinary Television*, Frances Bonner estimated that British terrestrial television recruits over 6,000 non-professional participants a week for speaking roles or as studio audience members. She notes that one of the characteristics of such 'ordinary' television is the inclusion of 'direct address of the audience, the incorporation of ordinary people into the programme and the mundanity of its concerns' (Bonner, 2003: 3). It is easy to see how this quest for the everyday voice is manifest in such genres as 'reality television', but what we will find is that this drive to draw upon the sympathetic qualities of the 'ordinary' is to be found in the structure of many news stories.

News values, balance and bias

Notions of balance and bias are central to the way we think about 'good' journalism. Such ideals are notoriously elusive, and Michael Schudson's (2001) discussion of 'objectivity' argues that it operates as a professional ideal rather than an inflexible template for everyday practice. Journalists are normally content to offer as far as possible a balanced and accurate account of events, in a manner that will engage the audience. Yet, agreed professional standards are central to much broadcast presentation, as they are across journalism more generally. This is most formalized where there is a 'public service' arrangement, such as in Britain. There, codes of conduct demand impartiality and fairness of terrestrial television news. British broadcast regulator Ofcom specifies that news be characterized by 'due accuracy and presented with due impartiality' (Ofcom, 2011: 25), requiring journalists to reflect not only upon the veracity of their story, but also on the possibility of alternative viewpoints in its interpretation.

But there are other expectations placed upon broadcast news that can be applied more broadly. In Chapters 1 and 4, we have spoken about the various sets of 'news values' that journalists apply in determining what should count as news, and deciding where the emphasis should be placed in the composition of the news text (Galtung and Ruge, 1965; Bell, 1991; Harcup and O'Neill, 2001). In his book on broadcast news, Martin Montgomery (2007: 4–9) presents a version of those news values, configured to accord with the needs of the broadcast conventions and its technological affordances. The following is a selection, along with some explanation of why they are particularly pertinent to broadcasting.

Recency/timeliness

As the plural of 'new', news has timeliness at its core. The development of 24-hour rolling news coverage has had a major impact on the way news is reported (Cushion and Lewis, 2010). As Montgomery points out, time has developed as an explicit part of interpretation in news broadcasts, with such phrasings as 'Today's top stories' and 'Coming up in the next hour', essential for emphasizing the freshness of the product and holding the attention of the audience. As we will see later, this imperative towards more frequent updates is also reflected in the expression of certain forms of contingency.

Conflict

Conflict is a frequently used criterion for selecting news, and can refer to rowdy sports events, neighbourly disputes and political wrangles, as much as it does international warfare. The newsworthiness of conflict stems from an impetus towards negative rather than positive news (Harcup and O'Neill, 2001), as well as the inclination for news to draw upon the empathetic potential of images of extremity and personal suffering (Chouliaraki, 2012). On another level, conflict allows the imposition of binary oppositions, such as 'us' and 'them', West and East, right and wrong, freedom and tyranny (Hodge and Kress, 1993: 162). Such reports carry with them visual images that need to be clear and iconic, often enabling the use of overt stereotypes.

Proximity/cultural relevance

As we will see from the examples we will look at in this section, broadcast news, in the same way as newspapers (Higgins, 2004), is obliged to highlight markers of recognizable cultural relevance, including domestic matters and culturally familiar regions and nations, which accords its own broadcast reach. Admittedly, a broadcaster that defines itself in terms of global proximity, such as BBC World and CNN, is more likely to carry stories from across the world. But even here, as Montgomery (2007) points out, there remains an emphasis on cultural proximity, irrespective of geographical deixis, such that countries with a perceived 'commonality' with the news provider – such as the United States and Britain – will feature more heavily than others.

Balance and bias in times of conflict

It is obvious that there are a number of underlying values that motivate broadcast and other forms of journalism, and we have looked at just a few of these. We are now going to look at the work journalism does to maintain normative principles of journalistic balance, looking at the contentious area of international conflict. When Tony Blair was in his final days in office as British prime minister in June 2007, he made a speech in which he identified the challenges facing the media. While acknowledging that 'the audience needs to be arrested, held and their emotions engaged', Blair insisted upon moderation and restraint, claiming that 'something that is interesting is less powerful than something that makes you angry or shocked'. Yet, we should also think about the cultural and regulatory constraints on how journalists can report such potentially fraught areas as conflict, and in particular how observing the 9 p.m. 'watershed' in British terrestrial broadcasting sanitizes how news may be expressed. It is remarkable to note that the now well-known film on J. F. Kennedy's assassination in 1963 was not shown on American television until 1975, lest it be 'too dramatic' and 'not the thing for home television' (NBC producer, cited in Love 1965).

However, the tensions around the possible internalization of this culture of expressive restraint against the appetite of the news public for gore and scandal are highlighted by Justin Lewis and his colleagues. They quote British reporters' reflections on how they dealt with the 2003 Iraq War, suggesting that 'reporters and camera operators in the 2003 Iraq War censored themselves, because they knew that the more gruesome scenes that they witnessed would not be shown on British television':

> Many of our interviewees felt that British television news coverage was too sanitised and would have liked to have shown more, whilst mindful of the need to protect children from the effects of such coverage [. . .] Guy Kerr (C4's managing editor) believed that British viewers will become increasingly suspicious of mainstream British news if it continues to be sanitised. (Lewis et al., n.d.: 14)

We will examine this further with reference to a report by the BBC's former chief news correspondent Kate Adie, on the American bombings of the Libyan capital, Tripoli, in April 1986. Briefly, the background is one of heightened tensions between the United States and the Libyan governments, which had led to journalists being despatched to Tripoli in the weeks leading up to the attack. Technology in 1986 meant that Adie's reports were largely pre-recorded through accident-prone telephone lines between Tripoli and London, or else filmed and sent back to London by air freight. There was little opportunity for interrogation of her reports at that time, but this journalist was severely criticized by the Thatcher government in Britain and the Reagan government in the United States for alleged bias towards Libya.

In particular, one report she recorded for BBC News shortly after the American bombing of Tripoli came in for extensive criticism (Higgins and Smith, 2011), but is interesting for its strategic focus on civilian casualties. Adie's report (see Figure 2.1) begins with a subtle but clear indication that she is subject to reporting constraints: this is a 'guided tour' (line 1) rather than an independent excursion. The orchestrated nature of this tour is further highlighted by her metaphor-laden description of the farmer as 'holding up his trophies for our benefit' (lines 2–3). However, she is also careful to draw attention to the wayward nature of the American bombing, using a shared lexicon of distance and direction: the farm is 'one mile north of the military base' (lines 8–9).

With the benefit of having seen her accompanying notebooks, we know that Adie altered her report to take into account a new story that arose as the journalists were travelling back to Tripoli from the farm to which they had been taken. This is indicated in line 10 in the transcript by the contrastive

A guided tour of the orange groves south of Tripoli:- the remnants of	1
Tuesday's raid, marked with the sign Texas Instruments. The farmer	2
holding up his trophies for our benefit, found in his chicken run through the	3
oranges and the olive trees a line of bomb craters. The Libyans have buried	4
their dead, and are dealing with the aftermath of the raid: there's still shock	5
– but much of the tension has gone – the official line is that they do not want	6
war with America. There are still many reminders, though. Including	7
several missiles and a variety of fragments and debris. Another farm – one	8
mile north of the military base – also boasting craters and crumpled metal.	9
But as we were looking at this, two small boys were being curious in a street	10
near the French Embassy in Tripoli; they brought a red object out of the	11
rubble – and took it to a young man nearby. He was shown to us on the	12
operating table. It's difficult to know if he's a victim of the American raid or	13
of the huge amount of ordnance directed by the Libyans at the aircraft.	14

FIGURE 2.1 *Kate Adie, BBC1 Nine O'Clock News, 17 April 1986.*

coordinating conjunction 'but as we were looking at this'. We can also see how the script has been crafted to encourage empathy with the local civilians: her notebooks show she initially intended to report 'two small boys were playing' but changed this to 'were being curious' (line 10). Such a reformulation adds a more human element in that the children are being accorded a positive and shared human quality using a mental process verb in place of an, albeit endearing, physical activity.

Background documentation also tells us that Adie and several other journalists were taken to the hospital where the injured man was being treated: the broadcast is accompanied by shots of the backs of the surgeons working in the operating theatre. As to the cause of the man's injuries, a gap is left in the coherence of the report between the retrieval of the 'red object' (line 11) and his presence in the operating theatre. In terms outlined by Dan Sperber and Deirdre Wilson (1995), the absence of explicit details leaves the viewer to apply the criteria of presumptive 'relevance' to the shift in circumstances, moving from the implicit threat of the bombsite to the scene in the operating theatre. Crucially, such formulations also comply with an internalized obligation to avoid explicit reference to 'gory details'.

The composition of this extract also tells us a great deal about the procedures of truth-telling. It is clear from Adie's notebooks that she was suspicious of the origin of the explosive device that caused this injury. Whilst the Americans had stated they had only bombed 'military targets', Adie knew that the Libyan armed forces were unlikely to have the specific device that was the cause of this injury. This is reflected in the strategic hedging 'it's difficult to know' (line 13), which combines the acknowledgement of the limited corroborated evidence with a personal point of view, here explicitly referenced to Adie's own mental process verb of understanding. While it has the appearance of a spontaneous expression of indecision, Adie's notebooks show this last sentence was the subject of extensive rewriting, and was therefore carefully considered. In the final broadcast script, the bomb raids on line 13 explicitly remain ascribed to the active agency of the Americans, while the possibility that the device might have originated from 'the huge amount of ordnance' (line 14) used by the Libyans is ameliorated by their use of such weapons in defence.

From this brief analysis, we can gather some idea of the problems a journalist faces when reporting a conflict, and how these can be dealt with using careful expression. Constrained by the censorship imposed by the Libyans in this case, Adie is not free to report what she wants from where she wants. This is linked to a desire not to upset the host government and thus risk expulsion from the conflict zone. At the same time, the reporter has to be aware of their audience and, in the case of war, the conventional expectation of a clear 'us and them' distinction (Hodge and Kress, 1993: 163). It was clear that the American bombing raid had largely missed its military target and had instead caused civilian casualties, the journalists' dilemma here was one of how to express the news in the context where the side we would ordinarily align ourselves with – the cultural centre of the news text and all its values and assumptions – may be culpable.

Broadcasting and sociability

It is clear, therefore, that broadcast journalism has to apply news values while, to some extent, balancing and feeding the cultural expectations of the presumed audience, and doing these things while at the same time discharging duties of impartiality. However, at the beginning of the chapter we presented the drive of broadcasting to present itself as sociable. We saw traces of this in the section above, when phrasings such as 'two little boys' emphasized the emotive qualities of the story, in a manner designed to appeal to the sympathies of the viewer. In this section we are going to take this a stage further and look at the features that broadcast journalism has in common with informal talk. Some of the main features of conversation analysis will be discussed, which will help us reflect on how these can help us understand broadcast talk.

When journalists address the camera or speak into a radio mike, they engage the audience as though they were addressing them directly as a collective or as individuals (Scannell, 1996: 24). We have already noted that the technique of appearing to address the audience directly is referred to by Horton and Wohl (1982) as 'para-social interaction'. While the para-social version differs from ordinary interaction in that it addresses physically absent others, it nevertheless proceeds as though it were subject to the normal responsibilities of face-to-face interaction: not least, to be seen as making an effort to be conscious of the feelings and pleasures of the addressee.

What this demands is the cultivation of a means of performing the journalistic function of delivering the news while calling upon the linguistic mechanisms of interaction. Figure 2.2, a short extract from the BBC Radio 4 programme *Today* (broadcast 31 August 2012), is an example of this as the presenter Evan Davis hands over to a special correspondent, Adam Brimelow, who will present the next item in the show.

The extent to which co-presenters are used as a conduit for the enactment of informality is notable. An easy mix of conventional face-to-face interaction with the co-presenter is apparent, one, it is assumed, that the audience will overhear, when Davis addresses Brimelow as 'Adam' (line 5); para-social interaction with the audience is seen when 'Adam Brimelow' is introduced to listeners as 'BBC health correspondent' (line 4).

Davis	It turns out it's never to late to turn to a healthy lifestyle (.) this is	1
	according to a huge new Swedish study of two thousand older	2
	people (.) healthy living (.) adds years (.) to life expectancy in fact	3
	five or six years (.) Adam Brimelow is BBC health correspondent	4
	and can explain all (.) Adam (.) the five or six years (.) was that just	5
	what you got from being healthy (.) when you were old or was that	6
	what you got when you were being healthy over your whole life	7
		8
Brimelow	Yes the unusual thing about this study it is it focuses specifically on	9
	people (.) who lived a long time already (.) people over seventy five	10
	[report continues]	11

FIGURE 2.2 *Extract from the BBC Radio 4 programme* Today, *31 August 2012*

This relative informality on the part of the broadcaster can also set in place a particular relationship between the audience and the news. In short, the journalist aligns with the audience in occupying the position of someone 'trying to make sense of' the news, and always looking to establish what the immediate impact of the news might be on 'ordinary people', such as the journalist and those in the audience. Brunsdon and Morley (1978: 87) describe this position as that of the popularizing journalist, who uses the language of the ordinary person against the obscuring and dissembling forces of authority.

On-screen broadcasting interaction and sociability

One of the key strategies of informalizing news is, therefore, the choreographed 'banter' between co-presenters. We now look at the importance of the news interview. Heritage (1985) and Scannell (1996) have pointed out that the talk produced by all participants in news interviews is not just for each other, but also, and primarily, for the 'overhearing' audience. Even where there is a co-present (studio) audience there to observe, they may only participate under very close supervision (Higgins, 2008: 53). At their core, news interviews, whether they take place in the studio or are a vox pop in the street, are for the benefit of the absent audience rather than for the interviewer.

In normal conversation, certain rules are observed, such as the use of adjacency pairs whereby some utterances expect an appropriate response. Harvey Sacks puts it rather obliquely:

By conditional relevance of one item on another we mean: given the first, the second is expectable; upon its occurrence it can be seen to be a second item to the first; upon its non-occurrence it can be seen to be officially absent – all this provided by the occurrence of the first item. (Sacks, 1992)

This can be illustrated by a relatively simple example, whereby a summons carries the adjacency pair of an answer:

A: Bert? [a summons item; obligates other to answer under penalty of being found absent, insane, insolent, condescending, etc.]

B: Yeah? [answers summons, thereby establishing availability to interact further. Ensures there will be further interaction by employing a question item, which demands further talk or activity by summoner.] (Sacks, 1992)

There are a number of tasks being undertaken by this exchange. As we say above, the summoner wishes to verify the presence and availability of the interlocutor, but just as importantly the exchange also provides a means of opening the exchange that is to come. We can compare this with the forms of sociability we see on broadcast news. This is the manner in which presenter John Humphrys introduces the BBC Radio 4 morning news programme *Today*:

JH: It's six o'clock on Friday the thirty first of August (.) good morning this is *Today* with Evan Davis and (.) John Humphrys

This is a greeting offered by Humprhys to the listening audience. It is implausible to suppose that Humphrys' words would be able to illicit a response (a 'good morning' in return) that would confirm the attention and availability of the audience, like the summons to Bert highlighted by Schegloff. However, the greeting does provide an appropriately sociable manner of opening the series of addresses that are to come. Importantly, this presenter-to-audience relationship is only one of the axes along which broadcasting sociability operates. The following is an exchange from the BBC Radio 4 evening news programme *PM*, where presenter Eddie Mair introduces an update on news from Cairo:

EM: Our world affairs editor (.) John Simpson (.) is in Cairo (.) it's quite a day John

JS: Eddie it's a remarkable day

Here, we see the presenter, Eddie Mair, shifting from addressing the overhearing audience with information on the whereabouts of the world affairs editor ('Our world affairs editor (.) John Simpson (.) is in Cairo') to opening an exchange with the journalist on location ('it's quite a day John'). The latter part of Mair's contribution is what Scannell (1991) describes as 'doubly-articulated'. It sets out the importance of an exchange between two on-air journalists, 'it's quite a day, John', in a manner that is designed to benefit an overhearing audience. Similarly, in the context of the programme, John Simpson's report is delivered to Mair, but with the purpose of giving a report to the listeners. There are therefore elements of the report that are explicitly sociable in the direction of the audience (e.g. greeting them to the programme) and other elements where the audience are invited to behold the enactment of sociability between the on-air professionals.

Voices in news broadcasting

It seems, then, a significant factor in broadcasting news is the incorporation of voices, whether that be on the basis of expertise, first-hand experience or ordinariness. In a moment, we will go on to look at another crucial item in the broadcast journalism toolbox: the news interview. First, however, Montgomery (2007: 144) provides useful categories for us to analyse the voices we hear on news reports. Aside from the main news presenter, there are four other categories we should think about:

- *The experiential interview.* Here, the interviewee can be an eyewitness to an event, or as mentioned in Chapter 1, the relative of soldier killed on active duty. We will see examples of such interviews in the report we will examine towards the end of the chapter.

- *The expert interview.* In such interviews, the interviewee is often presenting an expert opinion, such as a doctor who is being interviewed in association with a new health warning, or a university politics professor being interviewed about election results. Often too, such interviews are conducted with whatever professionals are involved with a news story, such as the policeman at the scene of the news story above.

- *The affiliated interview.* This interview is most often between the news presenter and a colleague who specializes in a certain area, such as health or business. We saw an introduction to such an interview in the exchange between Evan Davis and Adam Brimelow.

- *The accountability interview.* It is the accountability interview that we will turn to in a moment. Here, the interviewee is institutionally authoritative and can thus be held to account for the actions of a relevant body, such as a cabinet minister can be held accountable by the interviewer for government policy, or a company chief executive for a sharp decline in that company's profits.

These interviews do very different sorts of work in the news programme. Experiential interviews often provide emotional 'bystander' accounts. As Montgomery (2007: 178) says, 'in marked contrast to the accountable interviewee, [bystanders] are presented to the audience in a way that offers possible points of identification (or dis-identification), along the lines of – "yes; that is how I felt or how I might feel in their position", or even "that's not how I felt"'.

Broadcast exchange rituals: Arguments and sociability

We have said a great deal about the imperative towards sociability, and how this influences broadcast journalism. We will now look at the particular forms of sociability in the news interview. Turn-taking is a central element of spoken interaction. However, in multi-party conversation, there is the potential for chaos. Fortunately, as Deborah Cameron (2001: 91) describes, there are rules which exist to minimize this possibility in normal conversation. Such rules include:

The current speaker selects the next speaker

Or if this mechanism does not operate then . . .

The next speaker self selects

Or if this mechanism does not operate then . . .

The current speaker may continue.

In media interviews, however, these rules of ordinary conversation do not apply. In such events, turn-taking is usually institutionally predetermined (Heritage and Greatbatch, 1991), where the interviewer has the pre-allocated role to ask questions while the interviewee is confined to offering direct responses. A further point is that the media news interviewer does not usually express his or her own perspective or personally react to statements made by the interviewee. In order to maintain impartiality, the interviewer usually does not express surprise or shock. However, as we will see later in the chapter, the interviewer may adopt an alternative, antagonistic view to provoke the interviewee's response.

Broadcast media talk also differs from ordinary conversation in the manner in which it is sequenced. Sequencing is the order in which speakers contribute and the roles they adopt, and in ordinary talk this is usually not pre-determined. As Andrew Tolson (2006: 16) has observed, sequencing is particularly significant in media talk because it is so institutionally circumscribed. Roles are pre-allocated, the interviewer, the caller, the contestant, or the interviewee: roles which predetermine the contribution they are empowered to make.

Another characteristic of ordinary talk that distinguishes it from broadcasting is the long sequences of openings and closings. For example, in the case of a telephone call, the following would not be unusual (adapted from Hutchby, 2006):

1 [telephone rings]
2 Nancy: Hello?
3 Hyla: Hi
4 Nancy: Hi
5 Hyla: How are you?
6 Nancy: Fine how are you?
7 Hyla: Ok
8 Nancy: Good. What's doing?

In this prolonged opening sequence, the telephone's ring acts as the summons (lines 1–2). There is a process of identification and recognition (lines 2–4), including a greeting and acknowledgement (lines 2–4). This is extended in lines 5–8 until we reach the purpose of the call on line 8. As Hutchby (1996) points out, in most broadcast phone-ins involving members of the public, the first two moves in this sequence are unnecessary. In radio phone-ins in particular, the identity of the caller is announced by the host and the sequence is further curtailed by a much briefer exchange of greetings. The caller will then proceed to state an opinion without further prompting on the topic of the programme as the purpose of the call is clear from the context. A further characteristic of broadcast talk in this respect is the absence of a mutually negotiated closing sequence. The host has the institutional power to terminate the call – even cutting the caller off mid-sentence if it is thought appropriate.

In the case of most radio phone-ins that are predicated on confrontation (such as commonly found on 'shock jock' programmes and sometimes Radio 5 Live), Hutchby suggests the following four phases:

First phase: announcement and greetings
Second phase: extended turn in which the caller states an opinion.

Third phase: host argues with that statement, followed by a relatively free exchange of speaking turns. Disputed points usually make 'good' TV or radio.

Fourth phase: the final turn, the host initiates the closing which may be as minimal as 'thank you'.

The host has the final say, giving them the most powerful position in the interaction. In the third phase, they may introduce the argument and, as Hutchby points out, the caller is invariably treated as 'arguable'. The sequential effect is of 'opposition-insistence' and talk is orientated towards this. The caller's 'first position' in the sequence is always vulnerable as it can be argued against by the host. The host is able to employ a formulaic strategy to display this power – 'You say X but what about Y?' While we can see this is a form of exchange, callers are forced onto a defensive footing. This applies as much to the radio phone-ins of Hutchby's data as to news interviews with this in institutional power (Montgomery's 'accountability' interviewee, 2007). As has been suggested elsewhere (Schiffrin, 1984), banter and light-weight teasing are elements which contribute to sociability in argument. We find examples of this in many radio phone-ins.

Yet, in spite of these rigid structures of interaction and the arrangements of power, it remains that broadcast sociability is an important element of many radio and television journalistic programmes. As Scannell points out:

The relationship between broadcasters, listeners and viewers is an unforced relationship because it is unforceable. Broadcasters must, before all else, always consider how they shall talk to people who have no particular reason, purpose or intention for tuning on the radio or television set. (1996: 23)

Even where lapses into confrontation between interactants, broadcast journalism is obliged to be agreeable to the audience. As we saw above, the use of argument and confrontation can be a vital element in audience engagement. Yet, even when there is no direct audience link through phone-ins or live studio audiences, broadcast sociability can be maintained through subtle linguistic strategies such as the use of pronouns. This is illustrated in the following short extract (Figure 2.3) taken from the BBC Radio 2 programme *The Jeremy Vine Show*, which features a studio discussion between the presenter, Jeremy Vine (JV), and studio guests (TL and PL).

Awareness of the absent listening audience is shown initially in the contextualizing information the presenter gives (lines 1–2), to explain how there are three other people in the studio with him, but that the main voice we will hear is of their interpreter (the two main participants are both deaf).

JV	Mr Leechy and his wife Paula are both with me in the	1
	studio now here on Radio 2 (.) as is their interpreter (.)	2
	Susan Booth (.) whose voice you will hear (.) Welcome to	3
	you both and thanks for coming in.	4
TL & P|L	Hello	5
JV	Can you just tell us first of all (.) Paul (.) about your child	6
	and how you felt when you discovered she was deaf?	7

FIGURE 2.3 *Extract from the BBC Radio 2 programme* The Jeremy Vine Show, *featuring a studio discussion between the presenter, Jeremy Vine (JV), and studio guests (TL and PL).*

The studio is treated as a social space, where the guests are welcomed and thanked for 'coming in' (lines 3–4), helping to create a sense of ownership between broadcaster and listener. Vine shifts his use of the second person pronoun 'you' in lines 3 from the inclusive direction towards the overhearing audience ('voice *you* will hear') to the exclusive salutation to his studio guests ('welcome to *you*'), although oddly he is also excluding the interpreter, Susan Booth, through his focus on Tim and Paula. Vine then aligns himself with the overhearing audience in line 6 when he asks the guests to 'tell *us*', and thus includes them in the discussion. The audience at home are thereby invited to listen-in on an exchange at which they are not present, but it is made clear that it is for *their* benefit that the interaction is produced.

News interviews

Interactivity in the form of interviews between journalists/news presenters and others are increasingly being seen as vital to news reporting. The monologic report from Kate Adie that we analysed earlier was determined by the limits of technology at least as much as by journalistic convention. However, in terms of where things are headed, Hutchby comments:

> Increasingly, the more interactive formats of broadcast news are coming to outweigh the monologic contributions of the standard newsreader [. . .] Key agenda-setting news broadcasts such as BBC radio's *Today* programme or BBC tv's *Newsnight* routinely consist of a series of interviews, each prefaced with little more than a brief contextualising statement by one of the [presenters]. (2006: 121)

We have approached these developments through a focus on artful informality. Sometimes this is visible, such as the less formal clothing in-the-field reporters wear to make their reports on television news. Elsewhere can be seen a marked decrease in deference, where the journalist assumes an adversarial approach to their questioning.

If we begin by looking at how 'ordinary' language uses questions, we will see how different journalistic interviewing styles can turn out to be. In ordinary conversation, we tend to ask questions in order to seek clarification or information. For example,

Chris: How's your foot?
Tony: Oh it's healing beautifully
Chris: Good

As we can see, Chris's second turn acknowledges Tony's answer in a format we can describe as question-answer-acknowledgement. Slightly different to this is the use of language in the classroom where power relations are in operation:

Teacher: Can you tell me why you eat food?
Pupil: To keep you strong.
Teacher: To keep you strong. Yes. To keep you strong.

Here, the teacher's response to the pupil's answer forms an evaluation, and thus we have a format of question-answer-evaluation in operation. What we see in journalistic news interviews is somewhat different. For one thing, it is far less likely that the interviewer will use back channels such as 'Mmh' and 'Yes'. Also, the topic is defined by the news organization, not the journalist or the interviewee. Hutchby (2006: 126) suggests that the reason for this is two-fold. First, the primary recipient of the talk is the overhearing audience not the interviewee, and therefore less attention needs to be paid to such rules of politeness as allowing the interlocutor to stick to topics that will allow them to maintain 'face'. The interviewee is usually complicit in this orientation towards the overhearing audience, as they will rarely produce talk that is designed for the interviewer's hearing only. Second, it is not uncommon for news interviews to be edited for use in later bulletins where a 'clean' copy (i.e. one without the context-specific questions, interventions and responses of the interviewer) is necessary. What this amounts to, according to Hutchby, is as follows:

> The political interview is not only a mediated phenomenon in its own right – that is, a form of interaction that takes place in the public domain, mediated by radio, TV or newspapers. Sometimes, what happens is an interview becomes 'newsworthy' itself. (2006: 134)

The main type of news interview we will be looking at is the accountability interview (Montgomery, 2007: 146). Such interviews feature people who are public figures with some kind of responsible role in relation to a news event, and can therefore be held 'accountable' in some way. Montgomery has observed that 'accountability interviews develop out of a news item but also have the potential to feed into subsequent coverage – particularly by providing a topical resource in the form of quotation for a later news item' (2007: 153). He offers the interesting example of an interview that former British prime minister Tony Blair gave to the Al-Jazeera *Frost over the World* programme on 17 November 2007 (see Figure 2.4).

The following day, the global media reported this interview in such a way as to imply that Blair had used this interview to declare that the invasion had proved to be a disaster:

Iraq is a 'disaster' admits Blair (*Daily Mail*, 18 November)

Iraq invasion a disaster, Blair admits (*Daily Telegraph*, 18 November)

Blair's 'Iraq disaster' interview provokes storm (CNN)

Blair admits Iraq 'a disaster' (Al-Jazeera)

Blair accepts 'disaster' in Iraq (BBC online)

However, if we look at the transcript of the actual interview, we can see Blair begins to talk before Frost has finished speaking (line 4), and it is the interviewer Frost's words that characterize the invasion as a disaster, even then hedging the description with 'pretty much of . . .' What we should note, however, is that Blair does not use the word 'disaster' himself, but merely acknowledges that as an acceptable interpretation ('it HAS'). Thus, in holding interviewees to account, this is an interview style that allows a substantial degree of interpretative scope for the journalist:

Not only may the interview be held to account within the interview for actions and words prior to it, but the interview may generate material that can be used subsequently for accountability purposes. (Montgomery, 2007: 155)

Blair	[The Iraqi people want] the same opportunities and the same rights	1
	that we enjoy in countries such as this.	2
Frost	But but so far it's been (1.5) you know (.) pretty much of /a disaster/	3
Blair	/it it it it /	4
	HAS but you see what I saw to people is (.) why it is difficult in Iraq	5
	[. . .]	6

FIGURE 2.4 *Interview with Tony Blair on the Al-Jazeera* Frost over the World *programme on 17 November 2007*

'Neutralism' and challenging questions

The hazards that Montgomery alludes to may well be one of the reasons why so many politicians avoid accountability interviews, usually with the evasive turn of phrase that they are 'not available for comment'. Nevertheless, the currency of the accountability interview as a journalistic exercise remains high, and the position of high-performing interviewers as 'tribunes of the people' (Clayman, 2002) or 'public inquisitors' (Higgins, 2010) require that traditional norms of sound journalism are maintained. With this in mind, Clayman (1988) uses the term 'neutralism' to reflect the manner in which journalists' questions do not betoken a personal viewpoint but nevertheless challenges the interviewee. Part of the way this is done is through the strategy of footing shift. This builds on work by Goffman (1981). As Hutchby shows, a speaker may adopt one of three footings.

Animator: the producer of an utterance;

Author: the person whose words are actually being uttered (e.g. speech writer, a letter writer);

Principal: the person whose viewpoint, stance, beliefs, etc. the utterance expresses (e.g. a judge's words in a court judgement). (Adapted from Hutchby, 2007: 127)

As Clayman (1992) argues, the use of footing shift enables the interviewer to fulfil two professional tasks simultaneously: to be adversarial, while remaining formally neutral. Yet, argues Clayman (1992), this neutrality is actually a position of the truth-seeker on behalf of 'the people' over whom the power is being exercised. As both Clayman (2002) and Higgins (2010) note, this is a discursive position that warrants performances of aggression, acting on the public's behalf, that would be untenable in ordinary conversation.

We can see examples of these features in an interview between John Humphrys, the presenter of the BBC radio news programme *Today*. In Figure 2.5, he is seen interviewing Defence Secretary Des Browne in light of a High Court ruling that appears to suggest British armed service personnel have inadequate equipment and that the government is legally accountable for this.

JH	Let me ask you first why and presumably you do accept that the High	1
	Court ruled that soldiers were sent to war without the right equipment	2
	can sue the government using the Human Rights Act (.) you do	3
	accept that that was part of the ruling?	4

FIGURE 2.5 *Defence Secretary Des Browne in interview with John Humphrys on the BBC radio news programme* Today, *extract 1.*

Here, Humphreys is seen to shift footing from being his own author in the first phrase on line 1 ('let me ask you first why') into the footing of an animator whose principal is actually that of his interviewee ('presumably you do accept . . .') before shifting again to the footing where the author is the High Court judge's words ('soldiers were sent to war . . .'). This strategic play for neutrality allows the interviewer to switch between topics.

This interview also includes formulations by both participants. Formulations are inferentially elaborative probes which allow the interviewer to cast events in a way that may imply a different interpretation. In Figure 2.6, we can see the presenter (JH) formulating events leading up to the interview in a way that makes the government appear to have acted in an unfavourable light, whilst the interviewee (DB) contests this formulation, wording the events in more constructive manner.

Humphrys' initial declarative statement is directed at Browne by means of the second person pronoun 'you', indicating it is Browne's own actions rather than his position of institutional accountability that are being challenged in this interview; a formulation that is repeated in Humphrys' next turn. Browne responds by attempting to reformulate this himself by using the collective first person pronoun 'we' (line 10 onwards) to imply collective responsibility. This distancing from personal responsibility is taken further by the mention of the action being taken on legal advice (lines 12–13). Finally, Humphrys' unmitigated 'to stop' is downplayed by Browne into 'asked' (line 13), which implies a less high-handed approach to this matter. Thus, analysis of the accountability interview enables us to see how interaction in broadcast journalism is strategic in character, and dedicated towards presenting and

JH	You went to the court to stop the coroner of accusing the MOD of	1
	serious failures that is a fact	2
DB	No no no John I didn't try to /stop	3
JH	/ What did you do then?/	4
DB	the investigations/ will you please	5
	let me answer the question? I didn't try to stop these investigations I	6
	mean in fact I encourage these investigations and we support these	7
	investigations and I direct support for them from the heart of the	8
	MOD every single day (.) I raise the issue of cooperating with these	9
	investigations these inquests and we welcome these inquests (.) what	10
	we did in one of the seven points which were raised six of which	11
	were raised by em the the family in this particular case we on the	12
	advice of lawyers asked the court to give direction in relation to two	13
	words which were used by the coroner.	14

FIGURE 2.6 *Defence Secretary Des Browne in interview with John Humphrys on the BBC radio news programme* Today, *extract 2.*

contesting interpretations of the truth, while attending to such professional norms as neutrality.

Broadcast news: Managing the extraordinary and the ordinary

The accountability interview is an extreme manifestation of an artful use of interaction that we find throughout broadcast journalism. We will now look at how interaction can pervade the management of an extended news report. Figure 2.7 is an extract from an evening news broadcast, reporting on the murder and assault of a British family in France in September 2012. The extract includes the headline sequence, followed by the opening words of one the main newscasters.

It is apparent that elements of the structure of the story have things in common with the inverted pyramid model we see in newspapers. The

	[Headlines]	1
AS	The terrifying ordeal of two sisters (.) as their family is gunned	2
	down in France (..) one child sheltered on the floor of this car (.)	3
	the other slumped into the hands of a rescuer (..) but why were	4
	their parents and grandmother murdered?	5
		6
Translator	The role of an investigator is to find out what happened (..) but	7
	this is an act of extreme savagery	8
		9
Voice over	This is the ITV evening news (.) at six thirty (.) with Alastair	10
	Stewart and Mary Nightingale	11
		12
MN	The girls' father was Iraqi born his business involved satellites	13
	(.) whether that prompted a professional hit (.) or it was an	14
	armed robbery that went wrong (..) among the leads the French	15
	police are pursuing tonight	16
		17
	[. . .]	18
AS	Good evening she had seen her mother (.) father and	19
	grandmother shot dead in their car and her sister beaten within	20
	an inch of her life (..) yet (.) a four year old British girl had to	21
	wait another eight hours before police in France found her (..)	22
	she was hiding under the legs of her dead mother (..) after a	23
	shooting in the French Alps that has baffled the police	

FIGURE 2.7 *ITV1, 7 September 2012, extract 1.*

headline performs many of the same functions as a conventional lead sentence, specifying what happened and where. The newest detail to emerge – the discovery of the youngest sister in the car, after the survival of her older sibling – offers the hook for the story. The headline centres on the traumatic experience of this victim, with the incident itself presented as a presupposition ('as their family is gunned down . . .'). A similar emphasis, referring to the events through the senses of the victim, is then repeated in the opening segment of the main section (lines 19–20). The implication is that the audience will already know that the incident has occurred, and be in search of detail; provided here through an account from the (imagined) perspective of one of the victims.

This extract differs from print in the capacity for performance: to distribute emphasis (marked by underlining) to place stress on the drama of the crime (professional hit, armed robbery, within an inch of her life, shooting), as well as to emphasize severity (extreme savagery, dead) and familial relations (mother). It is therefore easy to see how a combination of the narrativization of the events – in particular, emphasizing the participants – and the careful use of emphasis allow us to gather a sense of the newsworthiness of the events. The colloquial nature of the language (e.g. 'gunned down' on line 2 and 'within an inch of her life' on line 21) used also creates a sense of intimacy and accessibility for the viewers. This is enhanced as the opening headlines are concluded with a response-demanding utterance ('but why were their parents and grandparents murdered?' line 5).

Just as the voice of the presenter, with all its stresses and subtleties, distinguishes broadcast journalism from older print forms, so the technology of broadcasting presents increasing scope to bring in a variety of participants, as extract 2 in Figure 2.8 begins to show.

The first of the outside voices we hear is institutionally sanctioned, when Mary Nightingale signals a temporary hand-over to European correspondent Emma Murphy. Murphy's voice appears over footage, and she anchors her position as part of the scene through the use of deictic pointers 'this road' and 'this cover'. Murphy then gives way to the professional voice of the policeman (captioned on screen and voiced through a translator), followed by two holidaymakers from the campsite at which the victims had stayed. This use of what Bonner (2003) has called 'ordinary people' to place the story in context continues in extract 3 in Figure 2.9.

The dynamic between the place of the studio as the site of control and institutional sanction (see Figure 2.10 and the various locations as sites of liveness and authenticity (see Figure 2.11) are emphasized by the shifts in broadcast setting. There are a number of points regarding this use of non-professional or specialist interviewees that are worth thinking about. The first is the quantity of such interviewees. Across the scene of the

MN	The family was from Surrey (.) Saad and Iqbal Al-Hilli who	1
	came to Britain from Iraq were on a caravanning holiday with	2
	their two daughters and Mrs Al-Hilli's mother (.) it ended with	3
	bullets to the head (.) not just to the family but also for a passing	4
	cyclist (..) our Europe correspondent (.) Emma Murphy (.)	5
	reports	5
		6
EM	They had driven up this road (.) a family enjoying a holiday (.)	7
	they were driven back down in body bags and vans (..) four	8
	lives snuffed out in an act described as gross savagery	9
		10
Translator	What I can tell you at the moment is that three of the four	11
for police	people killed were struck by shots to the head (. . .) we'll have to	12
	wait for the result of the autopsy from Grenoble (.) but three of	13
	the four were shot in the head (..) the role of an investigator is to	14
	discover what happened (.) but it is an act of extreme savagery	15
		16
EM	Beneath this cover at the far end of the path is Al-Hilli family	17
	BMW (..) Saad died in the driver seat (.) his wife Iqbal in the	18
	back (.) beside the grandmother (..) and on the ground just	19
	beyond (.) a French cyclist's life ended (.) possibly shot for	20
	what he saw (. . .) and amidst the scenery and the savagery (.)	21
	two little girls (..) an eight year old beaten so badly it was	22
	thought she was dead (.) and a four year old so terrified (.) that	23
	she cowered beneath her dead mother's legs so still that for	24
	eight hours no one knew she was there	25
		26
Translator	The girl was discovered completely immobile (.) in effect	27
for police	buried in the vehicle (.) behind the front passenger seats (.)	28
	under the legs of one of the dead women (.) under skirts and	29
	bags (.) completely invisible and not making a sound	30
		31
EM	The family have been staying at the Solitaire du Lac camp site	32
	(.) near Lake Annecy	33
		34
First camper	Just normal people (.) normal children (.) and they were just	35
	playing (.) the children	36
		37
Second	The people were on holiday (.) y'know (.) it's fun here (.) and	38
camper	somebody else (.) in the mountains (.) is crazy	39

FIGURE 2.8 *ITV1, 7 September 2012, extract 2.*

crime and the village in which the family live, five voices are introduced of which two, GA and JS, have particular knowledge of the family. Also, the sense of unscriptedness across these contributions is striking. Markers of hesitancy are prominent; a number of the interviews are edited to include the interviewees expressing their inability to translate their feelings into words. The main concern of the other interviewees is the ordinariness of the family and, particularly, on the part of the 'parent', a sense of empathy.

JB	Neighbours were struggling to believe that a family from this	1
	small town in Surrey had been so ruthlessly executed during a	2
	summer holiday (..) this is stockbroker belt Surrey (.) quiet and	3
	affluent (.) it was here that Saad Al-Helli (.) his wife (.) and two	4
	daughters (.) called home (. . .) George Aicolina lives <u>two doors</u>	5
	away and chatted regularly with the family (.) who <u>originally</u>	6
	came from Iraq	7
		8
Neighbour,	I had a tremendous shock and I am in a way speechless (.) and	9
George	emotionally shaken (.) ehm (.) because I have known him for a	10
Aicolina	period of time and I never thought (.) something of this kind	11
	would happen to him and his family	12
		13
JB	Jack Saltman was looking after their property while they were	14
	away (.) he said Saad (.) who trained a satellite engineer (.) had	15
	conf<u>id</u>ed in him about <u>problems</u> (.) but he <u>wouldn't</u> expand	16
		17
Friend, Jack	Err (..) he said <u>one thing</u> that may or may not be of significance	18
Saltman	and I <u>have</u> passed that onto the police so I couldn't say anything	19
	more than that	20
		21
JB	Saad Al-Hilli was fifty years old (.) although <u>originally</u> from	22
	Iraq he was a <u>British</u> citizen (..) he was a director of a company	23
	called <u>SHTECH</u> (.) that designed computer software (..) he was	24
	also associated with a Wiltshire based aerial photography	25
	company (.) eight year old Zeinab went to the local primary	26
	school (.) her little sister (.) Zeena (.) would have started there	27
	this term (..) parents were told of the tragedy	28
		29
Parent	It just feels wretched (.) erm cause I've got a little girl here and	30
	a little boy (.) and just to obviously hear the reports on the news	31
	on the radio that erm (.) what's (.) happened to the other little	32
	girl is just absolutely awful	33

FIGURE 2.9 *ITV1, 7 September 2012, extract 3.*

Importantly, through the correspondent Juliet Bremner, this ordinariness is explicitly bound up in location, 'this small town in Surrey [. . .] this is stockbroker belt Surrey'. Related to this is the relationship between national identity and place that pervades the report. In keeping with the expectation that the place of a news story be made clear at the outset, the headline (Figure 2.7, extract 1) places the scene in France. The opening contribution of the main report both specifies the victims (as yet unnamed in the broadcast) as British, before

FIGURE 2.10 *ITV1, 7 September 2012. Mary Nightingale and Alastair Stewart in the studio.*

FIGURE 2.11 *ITV1, 7 September 2012. Juliet Bremner on location in Surrey.*

emphasizing that the police – during an implied criticism – are French and emphasizing again the foreign locale.

It is apparent that such news stories use language choice and strategies of emphasis to highlight the salient aspects of the story and to amplify its emotive qualities. We can also see that location and identity has a role in guiding and substantiating the emotionality of the story. The extent to which there are a number of factors that contribute to an overall discourse of ordinariness is also apparent, and it draws heavily upon unscripted and emotionally expressive contributions from non-institutionally sanctioned laypeople.

Conclusion

In this chapter, we have examined the particular forms of language that emerge in broadcast journalism. What characterizes broadcast journalism is the scope for embodied and/or expressive performance. Across both interviews and news broadcasts, we have seen how types of performance work to emphasize newsworthiness and engender emotional responses. The language of broadcast journalism can also only be understood in the fuller context of the broadcast setting: the studio, the scene of a newsworthy event, or amid the stricken and bereaved. Throughout, we have also been concerned by how much broadcast news forms part of a drive in broadcast media towards 'sociability'. Within this context, we have also looked at the place of news values and impartiality, and how these might attend to the need to engage the audience while participating in the professional activities of journalistic truth-telling. We have been concerned with the peculiar form of interactions of various forms of 'interview', looking, for example, at ways that journalists engage others in a potentially face-threatening manner, finding that the engagement with the audience is discharged by the journalists' speaking on the audience's behalf. Finally, we have looked at how a news report can incorporate this sense of interaction from within a studio setting, as well as drawing-in outside journalists and other interactants in a manner designed to emphasize news values and maximize emotional engagement.

3

Magazine journalism

Introduction

Magazines tend to be more specialized than we find in many other media platforms. Both the demographic qualities and the expected interests of magazine readers are thought through in detail and placed at the centre of how titles package and sell themselves. Because of these possibilities of specialization and the forms of reader appeal in which magazines engage, the normative conventions of journalistic practice that we see through other chapters apply less readily to magazines, including even the inclusion of content that we might see as discriminatory in other contexts. One of the strands that runs through journalism and that we will see amplified in magazines is the use and reproduction of a sense of community, whether that be driven by mutual interest, shared beliefs, or a common national or regional identity. Indeed, what we will find as we proceed through this chapter is that it is useful to think about the language of magazines as extending beyond the production of community, and become implicit in practices of exclusion as well as inclusion: differentiating and setting apart their own communities of shared interest.

Magazines and synthetic personalization

In looking at how magazines use language to foster community, belonging and shared interest in readers, we will be drawing again on Norman Fairclough's concept of synthetic personalization, but focusing in this case on how the notion can be applied to written texts. Synthetic personalization is a way of describing how media text producers can employ linguistic strategies to encourage their audience to think of themselves as being addressed individually, while at the same time drawing them into a community of interest. As Talbot (2010: 151) explains, synthetic personalization has three facets: the establishment of commonality; the impression of two-way interaction; and the use of informal language as a positive politeness strategy. The commercial underpinnings of this strategy are clear from its roots in the advertising language of the twentieth century, as well as its continuing pertinence to advertisers seeking to refine their forms of address (Vesanen, 2007). In fact, magazine language has many similarities with that found in advertising, drawing as it does on strategies of synthetic personalization. As Ellen McCracken has pointed out:

> The special-interest magazines often encourage their readers to think of themselves as members of a distinct group linked to certain modes of consumption [. . .] Because of their commercial goals, the special-interest publications address readers with messages of pseudo-individualised consumption linked to the ideological roles expected of members of such groups. (McCracken, 1992: 257)

Given the supposed differences in gendered consumption practices as well as discursive communities, we will be looking at how magazines aimed at women differ from those with a primarily male audience. To begin with, though, we will start by looking at certain linguistic features that are common in most magazines.

Common sense assumptions

So what is the relationship between language and the construction of a community of readers? In his discussion of 'anti-languages', Michael Halliday (1975) shows how shared and exclusive vocabularies can separate and maintain a coherent social group: the construction of alternative vocabularies, shared used of metaphors. As Fairclough (1989) has observed, what are presented as 'common sense' interpretative schematics are required to make the fullest sense of many media texts. In other words, what do the participants in an exchange feel entitled to presume about each other's linguistic competence? In magazines, this can relate to the language used, such as abbreviations and elliptical references to the names of context-specific celebrities. Also playing a role are such conventional news values as recency and eliteness, as the magazines work to fashion their sense of community by referring to stories in previous issues, or by naming celebrities assumed are of specific interest to their readers (such as soap opera actors in many women's magazines and Premiership football players in magazines aimed at men). In this way, readers are drawn into a kind of complicity with the text. As Talbot (1995) observes, they are invited to silently acknowledge: 'Oh yes – I remember hearing about that!', or call or reflect fondly on similarly expressed stories from past issues.

Another factor for us to consider is the multiple range of types of authorship we happen upon while leafing through magazines. As Talbot has pointed out:

> Magazines are not homogenous, and they never have been. Diversity is the key characteristic. They draw on a wide range of genres and discourses, addressing their readers in many different voices [. . .] There is a consistent core of discourses and genres throughout magazines, which set up for readers consistent constellations of subject positions. (2010: 143–144)

While this is true to some extent of newspapers as well, these authors include not just the voices of journalists, but also those of readers (through the letters' page and perhaps personal columns), interviewees, advertisers and special correspondents (such as problem page counsellors, health advisory writers and other experts), as well as an encouragement of distinctive and quirky writing styles in more general feature articles. Sometimes, there can be clashes in the assumed needs of the readers, such as advertising for 'anti-ageing' products running alongside articles about 'growing old gracefully', or features highlighting environmental concerns a few pages from a section of travel pieces on the glory of foreign travel.

Many of these divergent voices and styles are determined by the particular genre into which the item falls. Figure 3.1 names some of the genres and discourse styles that routinely appear in lifestyle magazines for both men and women.

The distribution and emphasis of these genres and discourses will depend on the magazine's editorial policy and the perceived audience. For example, women's magazines are routinely composed and edited with the assumption that readers will be interested in relationships and so will devote space to horoscopes and personal columns which combine the discourses of family, health and the empowering drive of feminism. Men's magazines, on the other hand, are more likely to call upon discourses of health and science using the discourse of the advisory feature. Also, it would be rare for a magazine directed at men to include horoscopes dedicated to offering advice on the personal life of the reader. In ways that we will explore in more detail shortly, this can be linked to series of suppositions about gendered stereotypes.

Such underlying assumptions about differences between men and women can also underpin the more explicit common sense assumptions found in magazines. There has been a lot of research into women's magazines (such as McCracken, 1992 and Talbot, 2010), supplemented by a growing body of

Genres	Editorial
	Letters page
	Instructional feature
	Advisory feature
	Fiction
	'True' stories
	Reviews
	Horoscopes
	Personal columns
	Advertisements
Discourses	Journalism
	Economics
	Family
	Fashion
	Science
	Feminism
	Sport
	Environmentalism
	Medicine and health
	Consumerism

FIGURE 3.1 *Genres and discourse styles that routinely appear in lifestyle magazines for both men and women.*

work into men's magazines, with a particular focus on the development in the United Kingdom of mainstream magazines for men in the 1990s (such as Jackson, Stephenson and Brookes, 2001 and Benwell, 2003).

Long-standing gender stereotypes inform the content of such magazines in a largely unchallenged way. This involves a polarity of features which appear to produce a 'two cultures' view of male and female attributes (see Cameron, 2006). Clumsy as the oppositions may appear, these can be tabulated (see Figure 3.2), drawing on the work of Jennifer Coates (1995, 1996) and Deborah Tannen (1991, 1995).

The topics that emerge from the application of these stereotypes to women cluster around supposed interested in relationships and family, in sharing problems (intimate issues such as health as well as clothing) and issues such as domestic economy and management. For men, on the other hand, topics that prevail include competitive sport, muscle-building and toning and individualizing technological gadgetry; all underpinned by a knowing humour that removes them from the realm of intimacy and into a more publicly generous performance of easy-going camaraderie. Mike Soutar, the first editor of *FHM*, commented that his publication 'understood how men communicate,

Female	Male
Sympathy	Problem-solving
Listening	Lecturing
Rapport	Report
Connection	Status
Supportive	Oppositional
Intimacy	Independence
Cooperation	Competition
Submissive	Powerful

FIGURE 3.2 *Stereotyped Male and female attributes.*

and principally that's through humour [. . .] In a group of men there's no-one more respected than the funniest guy' (in Varley, 1999). As Benwell (2004: 5), too, has noted, 'humour is clearly a prerequisite of magazine masculinity, and it decorates almost every article and picture in a relentless way'. We will see examples of this when we go on to look at *Loaded*, but for now we can relate this to Brown and Levison's (1987) theory of politeness, whereby humour provides a marker of solidarity and thus emphasises the discursive community of the magazine and the men who read and enjoy it. Although the humorous tone is confined to selected areas of the magazine, as Benwell suggests, humour figures more as a unifying strategy in so-called lads mags than in women's magazines.

Positioning reader 1: The ethical woman

To help us understand magazine journalism, we will begin by looking at the editors' letters from two different magazines to investigate how their communities of readers are created. As Brown and Gilman (1960) argue, the solidarity of much of the expression of community rests on the strategic use of such pronouns as 'you' and especially 'we'. In keeping with Fairclough's (2001: 52) theory of synthetic personalization – that is, a drive to address unseen mass audiences in the sympathetic tones of individual conversation – we will look at how pronouns are employed to include the reader, as well as the role of presupposition and humour.

The first piece we will look at (Figure 3.3) is the editor's address to the readers from the monthly woman's magazine *Marie Claire*, a publication with a demographic target audience of women aged between 30 and 45 (Gauntlett, 2002). As we would find in most magazines, the editor's letter appears near the front of each issue. It performs the instrumental function of setting out the contents of that issue (in case a potential customer looks only at this page before making a purchasing decision), as well as serving as a greeting. It therefore provides a welcome speech that helps to create a sense of community and engagement by highlighting topics that are presumed to be of shared interest. The issue we are looking at is the final issue of the year and so has an added retrospective function, calling upon the shared memory of the magazine and its readers:

Editor's letter

fashion with **heart**

AT MARIE CLAIRE WE:

Publish stories that inspire our readers to make responsible consumer choices.

Raise awareness of inspirational women whose voices aren't otherwise heard.

Encourage our readers and advertisers to reduce, recycle or reuse.

Recycle in the office.

Avoid taking unnecessary flights.

Inform our readers about fair and ethically traded products.

Print Marie Claire on sustainable paper.

Offer cover gifts that are sourced from responsible suppliers.

Believe that by making small changes, together we can make big differences.

Attach cover gifts to the magazine using biodegradable plastic.

Let's make a start
fashion with heart

THIS WILL SURELY BE REMEMBERED AS THE YEAR THE WORLD DEVELOPED its collective conscience. **Ethical consumerism, eco trends and corporate responsibility** have all spilled into mainstream sensibility. Fantastically, *you* are the reason for this fundamental shift in behaviour. Global businesses are finally responding to women's demands for fairer trade, locally sourced, seasonal food and, of course, clothes that are not produced in a sweatshop. We expect the latest fashion at the keenest prices but **we want to be sure no one keeled over for the sake of our wardrobe**. Similarly, we are keen to follow a healthy diet but are willing to **adapt our taste to minimise food miles**. While celebrities, from Sienna Miller (see page 254) to Brad Pitt (see page 39), should be applauded for highlighting global warming, *Marie Claire* **readers have always led the way on thoughtful consumerism**. While maintaining our style cred (looking good is non-negotiable), our editorial embodies a 'fashion with heart' philosophy. We are especially pleased this month to join forces with **We Are What We Do (wearewhatwedo.org)** for your free gift. By flaunting your stylish tote whenever you shop, you will highlight the evil of plastic carriers and demonstrate the fashionable solution. Plus, you'll be one of the privileged few to own this season's It bag while partaking in the national anti-plastic retail campaign. Join us in making 2008 the year when we really *do* make a difference. **Wishing you all a happy and peaceful Christmas.**

MARIE O'RIORDAN

DECEMBER 2007 **15**

FIGURE 3.3 *Editor's letter*, Marie Claire *December 2007.*

Looking first at the layout of the page, it features a photograph of the editor, Marie O'Riordan, whose name appears at the foot of the page in a position similar to that of a conventional letter. The photo shows the picture of a smiling woman, who appears to be enjoying a joke with an unseen interlocutor. In this way, there is instantly created a sense of friendliness and light-heartedness, factors which contribute strongly to what Brown and Levinson (1987) would describe as positive politeness. To the left of the page is a column of bullet points that appear to be *minor sentences* (lacking a subject) when torn free of the opening clause: 'At *Marie Claire* we . . .' One such point is 'avoid taking unnecessary flights'. While it might be fanciful to suppose that this separation between the minor sentence and the subject (*Marie Claire* itself) implicitly recruits the readers to the subject position, at the very least these points amount to a 'mission statement' for the magazine and a rehearsal of the values it shares with its readers. Certainly, it is continued at length in the main body of the editor's letter. The use of lower case initial letters in the main headings ('fashion with a heart') also engenders a sense of informality, something that is emphasized by the addition of a heart-shaped symbol in place of the dot above the 'i' in 'fashion'.

Another important component of the letter is how pronouns are used. If we take the first pronoun 'you', which appears in the third sentence, we can see how this is directed at the readers of *Marie Claire*. This renders the readership more explicitly visible when it comes to be used as an *anaphoric referent* for 'women' in the following sentence. The terms of this inclusivity is extended to the production team, including the editor herself, in the following sentence where 'we' enjoins the producers of the text with the anticipated consumers. This mood of inclusiveness continues for several sentences until the beginning 'We are especially pleased . . .', which shifts the usage to be that of the production team, where they position themselves as acting on the readers' behalf to secure a 'free gift': a reusable canvas bag, which is clearly indicated as being a special treat for the individual reader. The reader then becomes the focus of the letter as the theme of environmental concern is extended to advocate the use of the bag as a fashion accessory (linking with the 'fashion with a heart' ethos mentioned above). The penultimate sentence is a combination of inclusive and exclusive pronouns, through the initial exclusive use of 'us' to the inclusiveness of joint actions by the producers and the readers in 'when we really *do* make a difference'.

We will now continue to look in more detail at how these pronouns are used in relation to the discourses. If we begin by looking at the general 'female' community this magazine aims to construct, as implied by its title, then we can see that the editor's letter achieves this in a way that ties it in with the more specific 'environmental' discourse explicitly advocated. The environmental concerns that are central to this letter are validated in the opening sentence which begins with the presupposition that this is common sense (triggered by the idiom 'this will surely be remembered as the year the world developed its collective conscience'), and setting up the readers as part of a community of conscientious global citizens. In terms of news values, this is validated through recency by the emphasis on this being a concern of 'this year'. The global nature of this claim is then made more relevant to the readership through an emphasis on their own contribution; the second person pronoun 'you' appearing in italics. The wider community of women within which the magazine readership is implicitly situated is associated with themes of environmentalism, particularly food, and the piece finishes with the common sense marker 'of course' in acknowledging the importance of fashion. This ties concerns of the domestic and personal realm with matters of global import, themes that the magazine continues to build on.

As with many magazines, 'celebrity' is a running subject matter that is presumed to be of interest to the reader, and this and other topics within the piece are linked to the social concerns that are assumed to connect the *Marie Claire* readers in a community of interest. Here, the celebrities named – Sienna Miller and Brad Pitt – are people who have high-profile international status and who appear elsewhere in this magazine. The seriousness of this topic is lightened by the use of parenthesis, in which the comment – '(looking good is non-negotiable)' – adds the humour of over-statement to the letter, along with the determinedly colloquial use of 'style cred' in the same sentence; a sentence that also provides a link with the 'fashion with a heart' mission statement on the left. This then leads to the 'free gift' of a canvas bag included with this issue. Any possible connotations of cheapness are downplayed by reference to this as a 'stylish tote' and 'It bag', also suggesting that the reader who uses this could add to the implicit campaigning zeal of the magazine's editorial stance to reduce waste. The discursive community of magazine readers is further linked with a wider community of assumed like-wise thinking citizens by the assumption that readers who use this bag will be participants in a national environmental campaign. There are no further details of this particular campaign, which leaves a common sense assumption that readers are alert to the magazine's ethos and require no explanation. We can also see from the series of emboldened phrases how these environmental concerns are emphasized, before a tone of reader inclusiveness engages half way through the letter to assert these are long-standing concerns of *Marie Claire* readers.

This all adds up to a community that is closely aligned with wider national and global communities. The reader is assumed to be an active campaigner in line with the magazine's own editorial environmental agenda. This agenda is clearly that of a caring, sharing collective, through the slogan 'fashion with a heart'. Underpinning all of this, however, is the implication of consumerism being central to the readership, particularly through the compromise of the canvas bag to assist these consumption practices.

Positioning reader 2: The knowing 'lad'

It will now be useful for us to look at the editor's letter from a magazine aimed at men. We will find similarities in terms of strategies of inclusion, but a number of key differences in the construction of the target readership. The magazine is *Loaded*, which is aimed at men in the age group 18–25 years. This is one of the first monthly lifestyle magazines aimed at men and first appeared in Britain in 1994. Other magazines, similarly directed, appeared at roughly the same time and more recently cheaper, weekly magazines such as *Zoo* and *Nuts* have arrived on the market (both appeared in 2007) seeking to appeal to a slightly younger demography. Indeed, *Loaded* itself altered its editorial stance to accommodate a younger demography after its sale by IPC to Vitality Publishing in 2010.

Such magazines as *Loaded* are commonly referred to as 'lads' mags, which Imelda Whelehan (2000) argues is an attempt to override feminist advances through the promotion of a laddish world in which women are sex objects and changes in gender roles are dismissed through irony. Mike Soutar, the first editor of another early lads' mag, *FHM*, claimed in an interview that the key to the success of such magazines is their understanding that men communicate principally through humour; something we touched upon earlier. The archetype of such a man, Soutar suggests, is in his twenties 'when part of you wants to settle down and get a mortgage, but part of you thinks your mates are more important and you want to shag anything that moves' (Varley, 1999). As we will see in an editor's letter from 2007 (Figure 3.4), this irreverent and sexualized humour is prevalent throughout such magazines.

This letter, as we can see, features a picture of the writer occupying a similar position to the one in *Marie Claire*, but includes other images of the editor which link in with the narrative of the letter itself. The signature picture of the editor shows a conspicuously laid-back young man, wearing sunglasses and puffing on a cigarette: an act which is itself marginally subversive in the wake of anti-smoking legislation in Britain. The tag line associated with the piece – 'always a pleasure' – adds to this relaxed and confident appeal, implying a response to the readers' thanks for producing the magazine and his delight in addressing a readership that shares his priorities and sense of fun. The letter itself appears with a signature at the bottom which again appeals to this matey, colloquial presentation, using the editor's nickname, Daubs, rather than the formality of the full name we saw in *Marie Claire*.

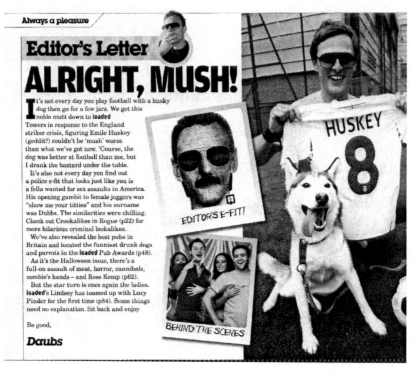

Always a pleasure

Editor's Letter

ALRIGHT, MUSH!

It's not every day you play football with a husky dog then go for a few jars. We got this noble mutt down to **loaded** Towers in response to the England striker crisis, figuring Emile Huskey (geddit?) couldn't be 'mush' worse than what we've got now. 'Course, the dog was better at football than me, but I drank the bastard under the table.

It's also not every day you find out a police e-fit that looks just like you is a fella wanted for sex assaults in America. His opening gambit to female joggers was "show me your titties" and his surname was Dubbs. The similarities were chilling. Check out Crookalikes in Rogue (p22) for more hilarious criminal lookalikes.

We've also revealed the best pubs in Britain and located the funniest drunk dogs and parrots in the **loaded** Pub Awards (p48).

As it's the Halloween issue, there's a full-on assault of meat, horror, cannibals, zombie's hands – and Ross Kemp (p62).

But the star turn is once again the ladies. **loaded**'s Lindsey has teamed up with Lucy Pinder for the first time (p84). Some things need no explanation. Sit back and enjoy.

Be good,

Daubs

EDITOR'S E-FIT!

HUSKEY 8

BEHIND THE SCENES

FIGURE 3.4 *Editor's letter,* Loaded, *December 2007.*

The use of pronouns is more elliptical in this letter than in the letter in *Marie Claire*. The most common is the first person plural 'we', which is used exclusively to refer to the production team. However, this is not alienating as the writer is adopting the role of older, wiser friend who is sharing his discoveries with his friends (such as the best pub guide and the more surreal 'funniest drunk dogs and parrots'). The opening paragraph invites the reader to share a joke with the magazine production team, linking this with the largest picture on the page: the editor sitting beside a dog and holding a football shirt. This paragraph explains the dog is a huskey (which is the name that appears on the shirt the editor is holding), and then puns the breed of dog with the name of an England football player, Emile Heskey. To clarify the joke, the writer uses parenthesis – '(gettit?)' – to cue reader involvement. As we saw in the *Marie Claire* editor's letter, parenthesis can be used to add humour and act as a friendly aside to give additional information that will intensify the reader's engagement, although elsewhere the parenthesis simply adds routine information such as page references.

The colloquial, informal language here again adds to the positive politeness features we find elsewhere in the article. The writer again employs a pun, indicated as such by the 'scare quotes' around *mush*, which draws on a common knowledge of language used to apply to huskies while punning on *much*. This is also found in the 'headline' above the main body of the letter – 'Alright, mush!' – which plays on its colloquial use as a term of friendly greetings (stereotypically male) and its homonymic relationship to the huskey dogs that is the main source of humour in this letter. Throughout, this opening paragraph draws on the common knowledge that readers are supposed to hold about the English men's football team's problems.

This paragraph is also an example of a lads' mags feature which Bethan Benwell (2003, 2004) identifies as the heroic/anti-heroic stance. Benwell has shown that the journalistic position in these magazines is one based on conceit of humorous self-depreciation; performed aspirations of heroism doomed to equally pantomimic failure. The masculine myth this column toys with is that men should be good at football, which is undermined by the admission that the dog is 'better at football' than the writer, leaving him to claim the small victory of being the more accomplished drinker. The theme of drinking is one that runs through this letter with its initial use of colloquial language – drinks are referred to as 'jars', and heavy drinking is celebrated in the capacity to 'drink the bastard under the table', with links to the feature about pub awards.

The self-depreciatory tone of the anti-heroic stance can also be found in the reference to the 'Crookalikes in Rogue' feature, where the sex attacker's e-fit image is likened to the editor himself, here emphasizing what is presented as a surreal joke by employing a pun on his own nickname. This is a regular feature of the magazine, and extends to a similar 'Pornalike' feature that likens actors in porn films with unlikely celebrities. Also in common with *Marie Claire*, further elaboration is deemed to be unnecessary as the community of readers are assumed to know what these features are.

Such references link with a common feature of men's magazines, which is their use of taboo language, here seen through the colloquial use of 'bastards' and the quotation from the sex attacker referring to 'titties'. The hypermasculinity of such magazines mirrors that in heterosexual masculine communities where swearing and taboo language is linked to anti-authoritarianism, and forms part of what Adler refers to as 'protest masculinity' (in Connell, 1987: 111). The semi-pornographic nature of these magazines, with their emphasis on photographs of naked and semi-naked young women in sexually provocative poses is hinted at here, in the final paragraph where the underlying assumption is that these images can be found further on in the magazine but that it needs 'no explanation'. The humour is far removed from the cosy domesticity of the *Marie Claire* reader, in that it glorifies violence and revulsion. This is clear in the validation of this issue covering the Hallowe'en period in an anti-climactic trope listing features on 'meat, horror, cannibals, zombie's hands – and Ross Kemp'. This collocation of repulsive images with that of a British actor who is well-known for his roles in violent films and television programmes is done humorously, but draws on the readers' knowledge of this particular celebrity.

The overriding tone is one of playfulness, and this is apparent in the language and theme. There is little concern with the outside world apart from the English national football squad. The community of readers is presumed to be one that has shared interests in sport, nude women, scatological humour and heavy drinking. As Mike Soutar comments, such a magazine is set up to engage with the sort of readerly subject position that revolves around the masculine domain of the pub, and deals in the humorous conversations that unfold there.

Magazine features

Most magazines have their most explicit journalistic content in the form of feature writing. There are many different varieties of such features, some of which are listed below:

- Service pieces, e.g. 'How to. . .',
- Inspirational, e.g. 'real life' stories of triumph over adversity,
- Personal services, e.g. make-overs,
- Relationships,
- 'Think' pieces, e.g. documentary news reports,
- Travel,
- Reviews of books, music, film, etc.,
- Interviews, often with celebrities,
- Humorous items, particularly 'real life',
- Hobbies and sports, emphasizing the shared community of readers,
- Nostalgia, e.g. historical articles, biographies.

  (Adapted from Hennessey, 1989: 61)

The type of feature included in a specific magazine will very much depend on the editorial stance of the publication and how it relates to the intended audience. For example, as mentioned above, magazines aimed at female readers, such as *Cosmopolitan, New Woman* and *Elle*, are likely to include features on relationships, lifestyle and inspirational personal experience, with celebrity interviews that will draw upon these themes. Magazines aimed primarily at male readers, such as *Men's Health, FHM* and *GQ*, will have features that place greater emphasis on reviews, service pieces and interviews with celebrities from the field of sport or film, all underscored with a note of humour.

In other chapters, we have noted how news stories have characteristic structures. Features are generally written to follow a structure of their own, as follows:

- Introduction,
- Premise or point of view,
- Thesis or frame,
- Body (the core of points/arguments/explanations),
- Supporting material (anecdotes, quotations, etc.),
- Conclusion.

(Adapted from Hennessey, 1989: 36)

Added to this, the display on the page will differ from that of a newspaper in that it includes a title rather than a conventional headline, which is then followed by the standfirst (the sub-heading summarizing the article), followed in turn by the introductory paragraph. This is often accompanied by a large picture which frequently takes up most of the first page of a larger feature. Subject to the publication's house style, there is also routinely a creative use of font and colour to draw attention to the feature.

In addition to 'news values', there are other elements which contribute to the composition of a feature piece, as explained by Hennessey (1989), Davis (1995) and Delin (2000). These are evidentiality, coherence and point of view. We will look at these in more detail.

Evidentiality

Feature writing deals with colour or in-depth pieces in a more determinedly subjective manner (Evans, 1972; Higgins, 2006) and the evidentiality often depends more explicitly on the credibility of the writer and other voices in the piece. Renowned or celebrity journalists or columnists give authority to a feature article, allied with the use of recognized sources. In large part, evidentialty is therefore established through these sources, and the greater the diversity of the sources, the stronger the argument. Such sources can include the testimonials of relevant participants or institutional expertise, as we saw with the experiential and expert interviews in news journalism. Sometimes, the authoritative source may be the acknowledged expertise of the writer. For example, a motoring correspondent or arts journalists would have a particular level of entitlement to write in their own voice. However, more routinely, features are based on independent research such as interviews, news cuttings, books and on-line resources.

Further, the diversity of sources which add weight to the authority of a magazine feature's evidentiality needs to be managed in such a way that their derivation remains clear to the reader. The more reputable or impressive a source, the more beneficial it will be. So it is usually the case that lengthy noun phrases are used to introduce sources, pre-modifying a person's name with details of their authority, such as 'creative director of Chanel Cosmetics, Peter Phillips, tells me . . .' (*Grazia*, 24 May 2010).

The words spoken or written by a source can be quoted in several different ways. A direct quotation in the form of direct speech can be managed within the feature by the journalist's choice of verb to frame the utterance. Quirk et al. (1985: 1024) offer examples of reporting verbs that can be used in this way: say, explain, insist, remark, state, argue, warn, recall or declare. The shades of meaning we associate with such verbs can influence how we interpret even a direct quotation. For example, this appeared in a feature relating to an athlete preparing for the Olympic Games: 'I'm a bit worried', she stutters. Here, the choice of *stutters* carries the connotation that the athlete lacks confidence in the context of the question and in delivering the quote. In a feature about vintage car renovation, the following: '"Not many of the American cars have many original parts left on them", explains my guide on arrival.' In this case, the choice of *explains* carries the implication that the writer was unaware of this potential problem and had to be enlightened, and also lends a mood of authority and truth to the quote itself.

Journalistic control over the utterance can also be exerted through the use of free direct speech without reporting clauses. In this way, the journalist is able to paraphrase part of the utterance, but leaves the reader to link this summary with the actual quoted utterance. For example, former Spice Girl Mel Brown was interviewed about her choice of names for her baby: 'Brown said she had thought hard about the child's names: "Angel, as she was my little angel through my pregnancy. Iris, as it's my grandma's name. Murphy, because he's the dad. And Brown, because I'm the mum!"' (*Closer*, 27 October 2007). In this way, the reader has to infer from the context who the speaker is, and thus the text requires greater reader engagement.

Greater journalistic control can be exercised through the use of indirect speech: thoughts or sayings are reported without quotation but with attribution to the speaker. For example, the direct quotation we saw above from the female athlete could be made into indirect speech to read: 'She told us she was a bit worried.' The process of converting from direct to indirect speech involves more than just removing the inverted commas to indicate speech. The addition of a subordinating conjunction ('she told us') is required to explicitly mark syntactic dependency, thus anchoring the quotation within the feature. There is also a stylistic need to change from first person to third person, so here *I* becomes *she*. A further linguistic change is the backshift in the tense of the verb and time deictic, which reduces the immediacy of the utterance.

This use of indirect speech allows the journalist to gain more control over the utterance, both in terms of editing for length and style. While the utterance may still be clearly attributed, looser connections are possible through this strategy and the paraphrasing can be vaguer in its source. For example, 'Sources close to the prince have said he is looking forward to the challenges of his new role', remove the utterance from attribution to a specific individual and place it in the realm of shadowy anonymous groups of people. Sometimes, there is no reference to even a vague source, and the attribution is stated authoritatively as fact: 'Most children have mobile phones.' Such unattributed sources are the least reliable and journalists generally try to avoid using them unless they fall within the 'common sense' discourse of their potential readers.

The linguistic choices made by the feature writer to strengthen the evidentiality of the piece and show the writer's viewpoint are reflected in the different ways of reporting this evidence to show distance from or alignment with the diverse sources of information. They may also be used to hide some sort of temporal disjuncture, such as an utterance that pre-dates the research for this feature. Overall, we can represent the use of evidentiality in magazine features through the chart in Figure 3.5:

Most immediate	⇒	Least immediate
Direct speech	Free direct speech	Indirect speech

FIGURE 3.5 *The use of evidentiality in magazine features.*

Coherence

Rather than just informing, a magazine feature will be expected to elaborate and explain: this is the 'in-depth' nature of a feature. The coherence of the feature refers to those rhetorical relations that describe not just parts of a feature, but also what it is doing. It is coherence that makes the text comprehensible, through the linking of arguments and statements. Referred to by Delin (2000) as 'discursivity', coherence relates to the underlying semantic unity by which the reader understands the text's propositions, actions or events to fit together. This is not something that exists in the grammatical structure of the text but in the understanding of language and context that people bring to the text with them. As George Yule explains:

> It is people who 'make sense' of what they read and hear. They try to arrive at an interpretation that is in line with their experience of the way the world is. Indeed, our ability to make sense of what we read is probably only a small part of that general ability we have to make sense of what we perceive or experience in the world. (1996: 126)

An example of this reliance on the knowledge of readers to bring understanding to the text can be found in the standfirst to a feature about the wife of the founder of the mail-order business, Boden:

> Sophie Boden talks about the highs and loves of married life with the man behind *that* catalogue. ('What it's like to be . . . Mrs Boden', *Easy Living*, April 2005)

Here, the journalist relies on the reader to make the connection between the subject of the feature and the founder of the middle-class mail-order company, Boden. This is emphasized through the italicization of the determiner *that*, providing a chatty, gossipy tone to the feature as if it were one friend reporting a conversation with someone of mutual interest to another friend. Without the background knowledge that such a mail-order company exists, this would make little sense, but having this knowledge not only draws the reader into the article but also makes them feel part of a community in which the term 'Boden Woman' is familiar.

Poorly written or edited features will have 'gaps' in them as those elements required for coherence are missing or are out of context. Examples of coherent elements to aid discursivity include the following.

Temporal sequences

> For example: *When* Price returns from the school run, she starts to tidy the house . . .

Contrasts

> For example: *Although* she has access to a vast wardrobe, she tends to wear only a few key outfits.

Cause/result

> For example: *After* a series of movie disasters, he returned to the stage.

Elaboration Describing an event/situation in more detail

> For example: Everett is comically glum about the sanitisation of show business – the military schedules of early nights and abstinence

enforced by po-faced publicists and all the 'hollow, vulnerable' parties that made him long for Studio 54's carnival of freaks.

(Adapted from Delin, 2000: 108; examples taken from *Guardian Weekend*, 29 September 2012)

These relationships of coherence hold the text together and provide the links through which readers can make sense of the article. These principles of coherence can be applied to any text, and not just a magazine feature; however, they are of particular interest to us because where these links are absent, the reader is invited to assemble the text themselves as part of the pleasure of reading. An example of such an outward breakdown in coherence occurs in the following example, which is a feature about the wife of the founder of the Boden mail-order catalogue:

She's the backbone of the family, juggling the needs of three school-age daughters with supporting Johnnie and organising their busy lives in two homes, in London and Dorset. *And* she's learning French. 'We have a theory that you have work, home and a social life, but you can only really do two. So we choose work and home. Our social life is shot to pieces.' (*Easy Living*, April 2005)

Outwardly, there is a lack of coherence between the elements in this extract, where the main elements relating to Sophie's role as home and family manager are disrupted in the middle by a the minor sentence '*And* she's learning French'. This does not fit with the rest of the feature, and the emphasis on the additive 'and' would imply that this is intended to be an elaboration that is noteworthy. However, as Grice (1975) points out, politeness proceeds on the understanding that particular 'maxims' will be maintained including quantity (which should be proportionate) and, in this case, relevance (see also Brown and Levinson, 1983). What may otherwise sit awkwardly and leave the reader puzzling over the relevance of this seemingly unnecessary detail instead invites the reader to marvel at the diversity and wonderful achievement of the feature's subject.

Coherence can also be used in magazine features to engage readers in a sense of community by elliptical reference to previous issues of the publication, with the assumption that they are regular readers rather than a novice or mere occasional reader. In terms of the understanding required to engage in magazine discourse as a competent reader, it is important that the relevance of such forays be clear to any practiced reader.

Point of view

Part of the function of magazine features is that they convey an opinion rather than merely setting out facts. This is one of the main differences between newspaper journalism and magazine journalism. In Chapter 1, we stated that language is inherently ideological and it is therefore inevitable that journalism is going to have elements of bias. However, in magazine features, the journalism is routinely emphatic in disavowing any sense of neutrality. This can often be identified through the use of the first person pronoun *I*, which, as we have already suggested in this chapter, is common in magazine features which can be written from the first person perspective.

Within magazine features, we also find a greater emphasis on the use of affective and experiential values. Affective meaning employs language which conveys a positive or negative evaluation on the part of the writer. This is often coupled with experiential values (Fairclough, 1989: 112), more often than not including the ideological or personal beliefs of the writer. As members of a discursive community, the readers are implicitly assumed to share in the writer's beliefs. Readers are led by the journalist's point of view into a preferred reading of the text. To return to the *Easy Living* feature on Sophie Boden, we can see here how the reader is invited to join in a positive assessment of the 'Boden Woman' figure:

> 'I don't feel I've got to be 'Boden Woman', but why would I spend good money on other clothes when it's all lovely? I'm going to make the most of it.' Sophie Boden's voice is muffled as she dives into her wardrobe to bring out another item from the eponymous clothing empire run by her husband. Who could argue, really? The Boden catalogue, ubiquitous in middle-class homes the country over, is full of what Mrs B calls 'clothes that cover you up, keep you warm and make you feel good about yourself'.
> (*Easy Living*, April 2005)

The discursive community, as we saw in the editors' letters, is one in which there are shared values and points of view. In this feature, we can see a continuation of the gossipy, chatty tone, with the journalist and the interviewee apparently sitting in Sophie's bedroom going through her wardrobe. The free indirect speech of Sophie, promoting the clothing range ('why would I spend good money on other clothes?'), is followed up by the journalist with a question directed at the reader – 'who could argue, really' – invoking a sense of agreement and complicity. This sense of informal collusion is further enhanced by the use of the colloquial 'Mrs B' to refer to Sophie when quoting from her directly, as she continues her praise for her clothing range.

Conclusion

As we said at the introduction to this chapter, the craft of magazine journalism is writing on a specialized topic to an interested and specialized audience. Even where magazines are concerned with broader matters of popular culture and celebrity gossip, a sense of community of reading and common purpose is central to magazine writing. In this chapter we have tried to outline some of the ways in which we can look at this. Concentrating on gender, we found that different magazines address quite divergent readers, assuming quite different sets of values and preferred styles of engagement. It will certainly be possible and interesting for readers to extend this analysis beyond gender, to examine magazines aimed at hobbyists, interest groups, political constituencies and music and cultural consumers. By mapping out the key factors of evidentiality, coherence and point of view, we have stressed the importance of seeing the underlying discourses of magazine coverage in terms different from those in most other forms of journalism, with a particular emphasis on personalization and subjective forms of writing, and how these operate to cultivate shared beliefs and values between journalists and readers.

4

Newspaper journalism

Introduction

In this chapter, we will be looking at the language of newspapers. We will reflect upon the structure of a news story, beginning with the essential role of the headline in drawing attention to and priming the story, before discussing the importance of news values and their emphasis. We will stress the role of news values as determining professional and compositional practice, looking at the example of celebrity coverage. Two matters the chapter will be particularly concerned with highlighting will be the distinctions in the use of language between 'quality' and 'popular' newspapers, looking at how the same story is covered across two different titles, and the place of gender in newspaper discourse.

News values as everyday practice

The order of priorities, emphasis and manner of expression we find in a news story are determined by those 'news values' we looked at in Chapter 1; that is, the criteria by which stories 'count' as news. In the Introduction, we first looked at a list of news values that incorporated the original list by Galtung and Ruge (1965) with recent additions by Bell (1991) and Harcup and O'Neill (2001).

As Stuart Allan (2010: 72) points out, these terms of selection draw upon the professional and lived environment of the journalist in a way that extends even beyond the stated criteria of 'cultural relevance'. This is important, since Hall et al. (1978: 54) remind us that:

Things are newsworthy because they represent the changefulness, the unpredictability and the conflictual nature of the world. But such events cannot be allowed to remain in the limbo of the 'random' they must be brought within the horizon of the 'meaningful'. This bringing of events within the realms of meaning means, in essence, referring unusual and unexpected events to the 'maps of meaning' which already form the basis of cultural knowledge, into which the social world is already 'mapped'.

These grammars of meaning and interpretation are not only social, however, but also form part of professional practice. In this way, and guided by the compositional requirements of that particular edition (Galtung and Ruge, 1965), we find newspapers routinely divided into specific sections dedicated to Home News, World News, Sport, Celebrity, Entertainment, Politics, Business, Health and Science, Lifestyle and Fashion and so on. In the larger papers, each section will have a dedicated reporter who will specialize in that area, although often the same journalists will be asked to produce copy across a number of sections, employing appropriately variant styles.

Occasionally, a story will also appear in the same newspaper in different sections, as its potential for engaging different news values is such that it may be deemed to merit separate coverage. For example, the England men's football team playing an international match will appear in the Sports section, but also may appear on the front page as 'home news' if there is some element such as unexpectedness or negativity that propels it into the realm of domestic or international news. Similarly, the oil spill in the Gulf of Mexico in the summer of 2010 was reported in the 'business section' in relation to the financial implications for the future of BP's shares, but also appeared in the 'science' section of many papers in reports about the environmental damage of the oil spill, highlighting negativity, unexpectedness and superlativity ('the biggest oil spill in US history'). Indeed, the story also reached the front pages when the US president got involved and was perceived as drawing on anti-British discourses, which took on news values of negativity, unexpectedness and, most relevant for many right-wing British newspapers, proximity, with the perceived attack on Britain and Britishness being articulated.

As Harcup (2009: 48) points out, knowing how to apply news values appropriately is a key professional skill of the journalist. The manner in which these values are expressed offers insight into not only the dominant social mores at any given moment in time, but also the priorities of the news room.

Headlines

So once a story is selected for inclusion, how should we set about understanding its composition? The headline in a newspaper is the hook that attracts readers to pick up the paper or pause at that page. In national papers particularly, headlines are usually written by the subeditor, not the journalist whose story it accompanies. The subeditor is skilled in using language to attract attention to a story, often sharing the motives of advertising to amuse and beguile the reader. One specific feature of newspaper headlines, though, is the fact that the conventions of page layout demand that headlines be in a large, eye-catching font. Because of this, there are space constraints that mean news headlines tend to employ words of seven letters or fewer. This leads to a special 'news headline register', where certain longer words and phrases are lexicalised in shorter words which are rarely used outside of this genre. These are often chosen by subeditors for their emotive, playful or informal connotations. For example, in British newspapers, verbs such as the process of telling someone off or reprimanding them is relexicalized as 'rap'. To criticize strongly is to 'blast' or 'slam', and to investigate is to 'probe'. Nouns can be relexicalized too, such as where young children become 'tots', and academics or scientists become 'boffins'.

Another feature of headlines is the adoption of advertising wordplay such as the use of puns. As Martin Conboy (2009: 19) has suggested, wordplay in British tabloid newspapers can 'often precede the strict news agenda as if a good pun is as good if not better than a good storyline'. This eagerness to have fun with language is not an exclusive feature of tabloid newspapers (the popular papers we will be looking at more closely later), but the accompanying irreverence and ridicule is rarely found in broadsheet newspapers. This wordplay is not, however, straightforward. Certain puns work on the basis of some words sounding identical, but carrying a different meaning and often a different spelling: these are homophonic puns. For example, the Scottish edition of the *Sun* used the headline 'Wendy's Talking Sheet' over an update on a controversy over party donations, in which aides of Scottish politician Wendy Alexander had distributed a 'crib sheet' to keep colleagues on message. 'Wendy's Talking Sheet' draws upon on an ambivalent use of an apostrophe (from abbreviation to possessive) and plays on the similarity of the sounds of 'sheet' and 'shite', particularly when spoken with a marked Scottish accent.

Another frequent sort of pun is the homonymic pun: words which sound similar and are spelled the same, but carry different and not necessarily related meanings. For example, in a story about a burglar who had been apprehended by a Polish homeowner, the headline was 'Pole Axed' (*Daily Mirror*, 29 June 2010), which draws on the literal meaning of Pole meaning Polish, but also the metaphorical meaning of stopping violently (pole-axed). It is the same word, but carries a different meaning and therefore an opportunity to fashion a pun.

Another technique often used in headlines is to use partial puns. For example, a story in the *Sun* (19 June 2010) about the amount of money being spent on temporary consultants by the government ran with the headline 'Dosh and Go'. The partial pun on dosh/wash which carries a colloquial term for money links with the informality of the newspaper's editorial style. This headline also evokes a well-known phrase used as the trademark of a brand of shampoo and conditioner indicating speed and convenience – *Wash and Go* – but in a manner in which the convenience is purposively informalized by the inclusion of the punning 'dosh'. The headline therefore primes a set of assumptions about the lack of care exercised in government expenditure, linking spending with assumptions over common and everyday greed. This is a use of puns frequent in tabloids, which, Conboy (2006: 23) suggests, politicizes journalistic language by directing popular forms of engagement at the institutions and personnel of power, and toying with the very lexicon of instrumental government.

Such a pun on a well-known phrase is an example of intertextuality. Intertextuality relies on a reader and writer sharing background knowledge of a phrase's or text's original or earlier use, and carrying this knowledge into the current use. We saw elements of this in the *Wash and Go* example above. Another example of this occurs in the well-known *Sun* headline (10 April 2009) which ran above a story about a senior police officer, Bob Quick, resigning within hours of being photographed carrying secret documents into Downing Street, inadvertently revealing plans for an anti-terrorism raid. The *Sun*'s subeditors seized on the police officer's unusual name in their headline: 'You can't quit quicker than a thick Quick quitter.' In the British context, this tongue-twister headline carries the same rhythm and linguistic play as a well-known jingle for a car maintenance garage, Kwik-Fit, which runs: 'You can't fit quicker than a Kwik-Fit fitter.' In the *Sun*'s clever wordplay, the partial puns serve to highlight this link with the original jingle while also passing judgement on the inept police officer, even if the adjective 'thick' carries the unlikely connotations of stupidity rather than the more obvious carelessness of the action. This intertextuality requires the very active involvement of a newspaper's readers, something that John Storey (1997: 130–134) argues is characteristic of the carnivalesque nature of popular culture throughout history, where the powerless temporarily enjoy expressive prominence in the poking fun at the mighty.

Aside from often-entertaining wordplays in news headlines, there are also specific grammatical choices that are part of the headline register. These often feature the reduction of function words (such as determiners, auxiliary verbs, pronouns). Most commonly, headlines comprise noun phrases, dictated by the use of a headword. A headword (Graddol et al., 1999: 80) determines the syntactic type of a phrase, and is the main focus of a phrase. For example, 'Cancer op tot goes home', contains the headword 'tot' (noting the journalese use of tot instead of young child) which is pre-modified by 'cancer op' to produce a noun phrase. To identify the headword, adjectives can be removed and the utterance still 'makes sense', although in this case the news-worthy circumstances of the tot would be lost. We can also see that this sentence is not grammatically complete; it lacks determiners such as 'this tot' or 'that tot'. To write this out in grammatically complete English, the headline would read something along the lines of: 'A young child who had had surgery for cancer goes home' (the phrase 'goes home' is also a colloquial rendering of the longer phrase 'is released from hospital after treatment'). Here, we have added a determiner 'a' and added tense with the auxiliary verbs 'had had', whilst also altering the syntax, primarily to avoid adjectival pre-modification. As we can see, the original headline is much shorter, yet still provides a clear indication of the associated story – to the seasoned headline reader, that is.

We have just commented on the importance of attaching adjectives to noun phrases, without which the tot's situation would have been unclear. But it is worth saying a little more on the importance of such descriptions in headlines, particularly in how the processes of distillation of meaning they embody can reduce the nuance of a story. The reduction of words in a headline can lead to a noun phrase, distant from the interpretative subtleties of spoken language and heavy in judgement. For example, 'A strange, lonely and troubling death' was the headline to Jan Moir's *Daily Mail* column about the death of pop star Stephen Gately (16 October 2009). Here, the noun 'death' is pre-modified with three adjectives. As Coulthard (1996) has pointed out, in spoken language we do not tend to use more than two adjectives to pre-modify a noun. Here, where the noun phrase comprised the entire headline, the series of negative adjectives amplifies the mood of negative evaluation of the singer's death that the column went on to develop.

The alleged homophobia underpinning Moir's article provoked a great deal of media comment, such as the *Guardian* headline (17 October 2009): 'Tabloid columnist's take on death of gay icon provokes record level of complaints.' Here, the noun phrase 'Tabloid columnist's take' is a journalistic contraction of the phrase 'The *Daily Mail* journalist Jan Moir's version'. Reference to Gately as an 'icon' also indicates a more sympathetic representation of the singer by this broadsheet newspaper.

The production of pithy and attractive headlines is one of the key skills of a subeditor. There is, as any newspaper editor will attest, an 'art' to writing the headline: it is the headline that gets the readers' attention and pulls them into the story. We have pointed out how the strategies of headline production engage the seasoned newspaper reader in an intertextual game, where popular cultural tropes can be used to situate a story within an immediately recognizable cultural context, and prick the pretences of power. Yet, dangers lurk. Cutting through the nuances of a story has the potential to reduce its meaning to accord with our basest prejudices. In headline speak: 'journos beware'.

The structure of news stories

Just as there are conventions we associate with the news headline, so we find corresponding conventions in newspaper stories. According to Labov and Walesky (1967) and Labov (1972), in our use of oral narratives in everyday language, we routinely follow the same basic structure. This comprises six elements:

1 Abstract – a summary of what the story is going to be about.

2 Orientation – who it involves, where, when.

3 Complicating action – what happened next? And then?

4 Evaluation – So what was this about?

5 Resolution – how the story concluded.

6 Coda – that's it, story over.

These elements are largely chronological, and usually appear in this order. As Barthes (1970) points out, such oral narratives contain an element of suspense, which he refers to as 'hermeneutic codes': that element of any narrative that remains ambiguous and is held back from the reader under a point of resolution ('the diegetic truth', in Barthes' words).

If we take an example of a news story, we can begin to explore the ways in which such stories are structured, and how they differ from oral narratives. If we look in detail at a story that appeared in the *Daily Mail* on 9 June 2010 and featured the pop singer Kylie Minogue, we can begin by examining the chronological structure of the story.

Just peachy

Kylie Minogue is a gem in her plunging coral dress at jewellery bash – but only just avoids getting her heels caught (*Daily Mail* reporter 9 June 2010).

1 She only turned 42 less than two weeks ago, but Kylie Minogue managed to pull off a youthful look as she attended a London party last night.

2 Fresh from her recent trip to New York, the pop star looked stunning in her over-length, coral, slashed-to-thigh BodyAmr dress with plunging neckline.

3 However, she flirted the disaster in a pair of YSL golden platforms, treading on the gown more than once and nearly getting caught up in it.

4 Despite being well-known for being a diminutive 5 ft 1, the long dress and towering Yves Saint Laurent platforms gave Minogue the illusion of being much taller.

5 The Australian was the guest of honour at the Tous jewellery store party at their Regent Street branch last night.

6 She made sure she proved a worthy ambassador for the brand as she wore a large gold ring, bracelet and heavy earrings.

7 Minogue has been modelling for Tous for three years and has appeared in several international advertising campaigns for the firm.

8 Last week, the Locomotion star travelled to New York to promote her new album Aphrodite.

9 As well as appearing on several US talk shows, she also performed at a gay nightclub Splash with hunky underwear-clad male dancers.

10 On Wednesday, she hosted the inaugural amfAR New York Inspiration Gala at The New York Public Library, to honour her designer pal Jean Paul Gaultier for his contribution to fashion and his fundraising efforts for AIDS charities.

11 Minogue recently denied rumours she was suffering difficulties with her boyfriend of 18 months, Spanish model Andres Velencoso, 32.

12 Writing on her Twitter page recently, Minogue said: 'Wowza . . . love life rumours have gone mad.

13 'Please pay no attention peeps. My birthday was magical with AV (Velencoso) and friends.'

It is possible to see here how the chronology of this story operates:

1 Kylie has been modelling jewellery for Torus for 3 years.

2 Kylie celebrated her 42nd birthday two weeks ago.

3 Kylie recently used Twitter to deny rumours of problems with her boyfriend.

4 Kylie went to New York last week to promote her latest album.

5 Kylie appeared on several US chat shows and performed at a gay nightclub while in New York.

6 Kylie hosted a fund-raising gala last Wednesday.

7 Kylie went to a party last night.

8 Kylie wore a long dress and jewellery by the party's sponsor.

9 Kylie didn't trip over her dress.

We can thus see that the news story does not follow a chronological sequence. The events underlying the story are not described in the order in which they unfold. Judy Delin (2000: 18) argues that this is not a characteristic of a newspaper story, and directs us instead to a structure that comprises three main elements:

1 Headline (Just Peachy)

2 Lead paragraph (Kylie Minogue is a gem . . .)

3 Body (paragraphs 1–13)

As we can see in this story, the headline draws attention to Kylie's dress and the problems she experiences in wearing this whilst attending a specific party. The *l*ead paragraph compresses events and represents these as being 'newsworthy' in terms of offering an insight into the relationship between her age and physical attractiveness. The body of the story then expands with a detailed description of her outfit and its relevance to the event she is attending, intermingled with paragraphs relating to her recent trip to the United States. Finally, the story ends with a quotation from Kylie's Twitter page refuting rumours (repeated in this story) that she was having problems with her boyfriend. We can see that, while the headline focuses on Kylie's outfit, and the accompanying picture shows her arriving at the party and smiling for photographers, most of the story is directed towards previous events, particularly her trip to the United States.

Following this, the body of the news story can contain a range of perspectives, comment and background details. Who gets to have their comments heard and who doesn't, or whose comments are paraphrased is something we looked at in the chapter on magazine features. The use of quotations to support a story relates to the journalist's need to provide the story with 'authority'. In this story centred on Kylie Minogue, we can see only one quotation and that is from Kylie herself, via her Twitter page, and does not relate to the main story as in the headline. However, the relevance of this quotation is part of the intrinsic interest of the story: that a 42-year-old woman is able to 'pull off a youthful look', and has had a boyfriend who is 10 years younger than her for the last 18 months.

The relevance of quotations to a news story is similar to that of a magazine feature (we see this Chapter 4). The difference between a newspaper and a magazine is most often found in the recency of the story in the newspaper. Often published on a daily basis, stories in newspapers are expected to emphasize their currency (weekly papers are less obliged to do so). In the rush to get a story to print, the journalist may often need to furnish it with quotations from less recent sources. Whilst this may not be identified explicitly in the text, linguistically we can spot such quotations by the grammatical construction which allows for such a sleight of hand. For example, an indirect quotation that is framed using the past participle can indicate that it is from a much older source: 'She has spoken of her illness . . .' rather than 'She spoke of her illness . . .', which implies a close chronological connection.

If we look again at the Kylie Minogue story, we can see that it carries a feature of newspaper stories in its repetition of events. Her trip to New York is mentioned in paragraphs 2, 8, 9 and 10, while her appearance at the London party occurs in paragraphs 1, 2, 3, 4, 5, 6 and 7. The more consecutive thread relates to the main story, with the less recent story of her New York trip circling around this. This is typical of news stories, according to Allan Bell (1991: 99), even though 'disrupting narrative chronology is cognitively confusing'. He goes on to comment:

> The story cycles around the action, returning for more detail on each circuit, and interspersing background and other events. The technique moves like a downward spiral through the available information. This is, in fact, described by journalists as the 'inverted pyramid' style – gathering all the main points at the beginning and progressing through decreasingly important information. (168)

This 'inverted pyramid' structure of print news stories places the Labov's 'abstract' first, as this contains the most important elements of the story. These elements are themselves determined by how news values are applied within the story; what is regarded as newsworthy in one newspaper may be considered differently in others. Why, for example, might the UK tabloid the *Daily Mail* feature prominently a story of a pop star's outfit worn at a party, when the story does not appear at all in the same day's edition of the broadsheet the *Guardian*? Also, that Kylie had been taking part in an event that was part of London's 'Jewellery Week' is not mentioned in the *Daily Mail* article, but a story relating to this event does appear in the 'Business' pages of the *Guardian*. Here, the news values of the story are largely what are used to judge its appropriateness and worthiness for coverage.

Popular and quality styles

Of course, some students of journalism might suggest that pop stars such as Kylie should not be featured in newspapers in the first place. Certainly, the emphasis on 'celebrity' differs from one paper to the next. Across a number of national contexts, newspapers are divided into two categories that are occasionally problematic: the quality press and the popular press. A substantial amount of work has been conducted on the cultural differences between these two categories (Tulloch and Sparks, 2000). Of course, one objection is that the opposition plays out a hierarchy of judgement already established in the definition of one category as the bearers of a certain 'quality' absent, by implication, in their more 'popular' competitors (Temple, 2008). One way of thinking about the difference in practical terms is on the level of political engagement. Political coverage in the popular press is lesser both in quantity and depth than in their 'quality' press counterparts.

On the other hand, looking at the normative terms of this popular/quality distinction critically, another approach has been to see them as engaged in different sorts of discursive activity: related in terms of their commitment to the norms of journalism, but manifesting divergent priorities and offering different forms of appeal to their readership. Higgins (2010), for example, writes about how newspapers in the British context have come to represent various social groupings and interests, along the axes of social class, politics, gender and lifestyle.

It is the British context, and its sharp division between quality and popular (or 'tabloid' press) we are going to look at here; we will examine how two different newspapers deal with the same set of events. The context of the story in question is a British teacher who had fled to France with one of the schoolgirls in his care, and had been apprehended by police. This first extract (see Figure 4.1) is the first half of the report from the 'quality' broadsheet newspaper the *Daily Telegraph*.

1	[headline] X's plans for life on the run
2	X, the schoolgirl who ran off to France with her maths teacher, was
3	finally reunited with her family last night, as details emerged of
4	their final days on the run./ The 15 year-old flew back to Britain from
5	Bordeaux, where she and Jeremy Forrest were found by French
6	police on Friday, accompanied by her mother and police officers./
7	Mr Forrest, 30, remained in jail in the French city awaiting extradition
8	to Britain over alleged abduction after his disappearance with his
9	pupil from their homes in East Sussex./ He is expected to return as
10	early as Tuesday after his lawyer indicated that he would not contest
11	extradition proceedings./ The full details of the couple's nine days
12	on the run emerged including how:/ - X travelled to France using the
13	passport of her 37 year-old mother, X, according to lawyers present
14	at a closed court hearing in the city;/ - Mr Forrest used two false
15	identities, calling himself Jack Grant and Jack Francis Dean, and had a
16	French email account in one of the names;/ - he and X booked into a
17	double room in a two-star hotel in Bourdeaux, where the owner said
18	they were "discreet";/

FIGURE 4.1 *Continued*

19	Mr Forrest sought work in a French bar using a CV that he had a
20	degree in journalism and worked in human resources./ Questions
21	were also emerging in Britain over his conduct as a teacher, with
22	evidence that pupils at a previous school where worked sent him
23	familiar messages and appeared to attend performances he gave in
24	pubs as an amateur musician./ The disclosure that X was able to cross
25	the Channel on a ferry with Mr Forrest on her mother's passport will
26	cause concern not to British authorities – there are no exit controls
27	from the UK – but to the French, whose customs and immigration
28	officials are supposed to check passengers in all cars arriving from
29	Britain./ It also underlines what legal sources in France said was the
30	couple's determination to maintain a life on the run. The schoolgirl had
31	her own passport but it would have raised suspicions had she been
32	travelling on it without her parents./ Legal sources disclosed that Mr
33	Forrest – who married his wife Emily in April 2011 – told police their
34	plan had been to stay in France until the schoolgirl's next birthday,
35	thought to be next June./ The teacher had avoided using his bank or
36	credit cards for fear of altering the authorities to their whereabouts
37	and settled hotel bills in cash./ His CV also showed some level of
38	preplanning. He had set up an email account with a French internet
39	service as "Jack Francis Dean"./ The manager of a hotel in Bourdeaux
40	where the couple spent one night said that Mr Forrest had registered
41	for a double room as "Jack Grant"./ When asked where his companion
42	was, the teacher replied in an apparent attempt to avoid suspicion
43	about her age: "She's waiting outside."/ Mr Forrest and his pupil spent
44	Wednesday night in a small room at the two-star Hotel Choisuel,
45	a 10-minute walk from where they were arrested on Friday. They
46	paid €60 (£48) for room number 312 at the back of the hotel./ Erick
47	Hocher, the hotel owner, said they were "discreet"./ "What intrigued
48	me was that he came in alone, booked a room, and when I asked
49	him where she was he told me, 'She's waiting outside', which is not
50	how things are done generally." The couple checked out on Thursday
51	morning and a few hours later police arrived to interview the owner,
52	and inspect the room./ That day, Mr Forrest handed his CV to several
53	pubs and bars seeking work, including a British pub called HMS
54	Victory, near Palace de la Victoire and the Houses of Parliament pub,
55	which was advertising for English-speaking bar staff./ Nowhere on
56	his CV did it mention his teaching qualifications or reveal that he
57	worked as a teacher./ Instead he described himself as a "keen writer
58	and musician" and listed his qualifications as a degree in journalism
59	from the University of Northampton, along with GCSEs and A-levels
60	from Crownwoods College, a school in south-east London, including
61	a C in maths, the subject he taught in real life. (The Daily Telegraph,
62	September 30 2012).

FIGURE 4.1 Daily Telegraph, *30 September 2012, extract 1.*

As we noted in the previous section, the most important part of a newspaper story is the opening paragraph, and this one does a considerable amount of work. First, the opening offers a partial summary of the developments that led to this point, where the girl's name is immediately followed by a subordinate clause, reminding the reader of her role in an on-going drama ('the schoolgirl who ran off to France with her maths teacher' – lines 2–3). The human element of the story is emphasized at this early stage, both in terms of the status of one of the main agents, 'X, the schoolgirl', and in expressing her apprehension as a reunion 'with her family' (line 3). It also sets out the timeliness of this contribution to the story: an action rendered in the past tense of 'ran off' finds resolution in the more time-specific and recent 'last night', which is presented using the conjunction 'as' corresponding to the emergence of more information ('as details emerged').

The ordering and distribution of these further details is notable. In keeping with the loading of information and newsworthy characteristics in the opening paragraph, it is clear that the details become more adorned as the text of the story proceeds. Examples of this include details of the hotel. What is first expressed as 'a double room in a two-star hotel in Bourdeaux' (lines 17–18) and expanded to 'a small room at the two-star Hotel Choisuel, a 10-minute walk from where they were arrested on Friday' (line 45) including details of the room tariff. Also, what on the first mention is confined as 'Mr Forrest sought work in a French bar' (line 19) later becomes 'Mr Forrest handed his CV to several pubs and bars seeking work, including a British pub called HMS Victory, near Palace de la Victoire and the Houses of Parliament pub, which was advertising for English-speaking bar staff' (lines 52–55). Another example is the details of Mr Forrest's CV, appearing the first time as 'Mr Forrest sought work in a French bar using a CV that he had a degree in journalism and worked in human resources' (line 20), before the elaborated version, beginning 'Nowhere on his CV' and ending 'the subject he taught in real life' is used later (line 61). In the *Daily Telegraph* version, the details therefore become more expansive as the story proceeds.

The same story featured in that day's Scottish edition of popular tabloid newspaper the *Sun* (see Figure 4.2).

There are a number of key differences between the treatment of the story in the *Sun* and in the *Telegraph*. The most superficial difference is in the number of words devoted to the story: in its full form, the *Telegraph* story is more than double the length of the *Sun*'s. Yet, in spite of this, the descriptive language used by the *Sun* is substantially more expansive.

The *Sun*'s expressive register finds form in the references to teacher Jeremy Forrest. Within the classic tabloid lexicon teachers are referred to using the nominalization 'sir' (Spiegl, 1989: 75), which is here expanded in the headline to 'Runaway Sir'. Subsequent references to teacher Forrest draw upon such constructs as compound nouns, where references to objects and persons in

1	[Headline] GOT HIM/ Runaway sir in suicide jail/ GOT HER/ X jets home to
2	family
3	
4	Grim-face school teacher Jeremy Forrest is led into court after his eight days on the
5	run with pupil X./ The 30 year-old was pictured in Bordeaux, south-west France,
6	before X, 15, flew home yesterday for an emotional reunion with her family./ Forrest
7	was being held at the high-security Gradignan prison last night – one of the toughest
8	jails in France./ It houses accused killers and rapists and has one of the highest
9	suicide rates in the French penal system./ The Scottish Sun can reveal that the
10	pair had been moving from one fleapit hotel to another in Bordeaux before being
11	found. He was said to have been hawking a fake CV round bars in a search for work
12	while X hid out of sight./ One place they stayed at was the grubby two-star Hotel
13	Choiseul. Forrest checked in on Wednesday under the pseudonym of Jack Grant
14	and paid in cash. He was given the £48-a-night Room 312. It is drab, with a white
15	iron bedstead, stained red bed sheets and dirt covering peeling wallpaper./ Manager
16	Erick Augier, 48, said: "He didn't look happy. I wouldn't say anxious – but definitely
17	not happy./ I didn't see her until she walked past reception to go up the stairs. I
18	thought they were just a normal couple."/ Amateur/ Mr Augier added that the pair
19	"didn't talk a lot to each other" and were "not particularly amorous"./ Forrest checked
20	in on Friday, September 21, and the couple left the following morning./ Desperate
21	Forrest appeared to use another identity as he scoured the city for work./ This time
22	he called himself Jack Francis Dean. Barmaid Mairead Shortt, 37, said he went into
23	the Connemara Irish pub to be told there were no vacancies./ She recalled: "On
24	Wednesday he asked for cash-in-hand work. He didn't have a mobile number or
25	email address, so he came back next day with an amateur-looking CV, clearly made
26	up in an Internet cafe. It was only a matter of time before he got caught – Sky
27	News is always on in most of the English and Irish bars."/ The CV part-time musician
28	Forrest is alleged to have circulated claimed he worked in human resources at IPC
29	Media, publishers of magazine NME, and even said he had written for the mag./
30	Forrest – a maths teacher at the Bishop Bell school in Eastbourne – and X went
31	missing last Thursday./ They were picked up on Friday close to the HMS Victory pub
32	in Bordeaux. Forrest had been there the day before with his CV. But the manager
33	called cops, who swooped as he returned. X was taken into police protection./
34	Forrest wore a blue-and-white checked shirt with dark trousers as he was escorted
35	from the city's criminal court. He is being held at overcrowded Gradignan on
36	suspicion of child abduction but is not fighting extradition./ X flew home to be
37	greeted by her mum in a secret location. Two cops were with her as she boarded an
38	easyjet flight to Gatwick. (The Scottish Sun, 30 September 2012)

FIGURE 4.2 Scottish Sun, *30 September 2012, extract 2.*

the story are combined with an adjective in order to establish a mood or add meaning, such as 'Grim-faced school teacher' (line 4), 'Desperate Forrest' (line 21) and 'part-time musician Forrest'. This contrasts with the *Telegraph* copy which, after establishing the role of 'her maths teacher' (*Telegraph*, lines 2–3) and age in 'Mr Forrest, 30' (*Telegraph*, line 7) confines its references to

'Mr Forrest' throughout, occasionally followed by information-bearing clauses such as 'who married his wife Emily in April 2011' (*Telegraph*, line 33).

The *Sun*'s naming practices around schoolgirl X differ from these quite considerably. The 'Runaway Sir' of the headline is set against an accompanying headline in which she is referred to in an unadorned form as 'X'. After the initial, explanatory references to 'pupil X' followed by 'X, 15' in the opening paragraph, subsequent references use X's given name presented in isolation (lines 12, 33, 36). The naming practices in the *Sun* – themselves essential to specify the roles of each actor in the story – are employed to add detail and colour to the profile of the allegedly guilty party.

This style of writing in the *Sun*, where a briefer text is adorned with a great deal more description applies to other details of the story. One is Forrest's counterfeit CV, first referred to using the emotive term 'hawking a fake CV' (*Sun*, line 11), followed by 'amateur-looking CV' (*Sun*, line 25). Another is the hotel room the couple were using when apprehended. While the *Telegraph* contains its appraisal to 'a double room in a two star hotel in Bordeaux' (*Telegraph*, lines 17–18), later named in the reference to 'the two-star Hotel Choisuel' followed by room tariffs (*Telegraph*, lines 44–46), the *Sun* mobilizes mention of the hotel to add to the wretchedness of the situation: what begins with a reference to a 'fleapit hotel' (*Sun*, line 10) develops into 'the grubby two-star Hotel Choisuel' (*Sun*, line 13), and then elaborated further into the appraisal 'drab, with a white iron bedstead, stained red bed sheets and dirt covering peeling wallpaper' (*Sun*, lines 14–15). Third, and perhaps most significant, is the description of the jail in which Forrest is held. This is first referred using the compound noun 'suicide jail' in the headline (line 1), before an extended description on the conditions to be found there (line 8) and a closing reference to 'overcrowded Gradignan' (*Sun*, line 35). The association of Forrest's location with that of 'murders and rapists' (*Sun*, line 8) serves to align him with those guilty of the most serious and newsworthy crimes through a process referred to as *semantic engineering*. In this process the semantic properties of one set of signifiers (here, murderers and rapists) are aligned with those of another usually unrelated set to infer a shared meaning.

In discussing the differences in popular and quality newspaper style, Bell (1991: 105) offers the general observation that news styles are adapted to the anticipated audience in a manner analogous to a 'speaker shifting her style to be more like the person she is talking to'. It is certainly true that papers in the quality category draw upon a quite focused lexicon and grammatical style. But there is much more to the difference than this, since popular newspapers draw upon their own lexicon and style, associated with and peculiar to popular journalism. Using their own conventions of language, popular papers are more inclined to write in order to engage the passions of their readership. As van Dijk (1988: 123) points out, news values are emphasized on the basis of their likely relevance to the reader (consonance), with a preference often given to instances of 'deviance and negativity'. Where such news values are present, negatively charged words such as 'hawking' can be used to emphasize the preferred mood of the story, and generate and hold out the offer to the readers to participate in a play of emotional exchange. In the *Sun* version of the story, this is enhanced by the adjectival descriptions of the hotel room (lines 14–15) which implies an eyewitness account of a scene that highlights the sexual scandal while also removing any sense of romance from the narrative.

Gender

In Chapter 3, we discussed the creation of communities of readers through gender in magazines. We will now look at gender in newspapers: how newspaper content is geared towards specific genders and what this means.

Since Second Wave Feminism in the 1960s and 1970s raised awareness of gender inequalities, there has been a great deal of research on how women are disadvantaged in media coverage. Since theorists such as Dale Spender revealed English as an inherently sexist language, Second Wave Feminism sought to raise awareness of this and eventually the National Union of Journalists (NUJ) produced guidelines that encouraged journalists to think more about the language they used. The main elements of the NUJ's guidelines are summarized in Figure 4.3.

Many of these lexical items reflect changes in society that have led to wider employment opportunities for women, so now professions such as media production and business management are not exclusively male domains. Other terms relate to the assumption about female roles, such as childcare and domestic work. Newspaper style guides will indicate to journalists what the preferred lexical choice will be for that paper (such as the *Guardian*'s guide which tells its journalists to use 'actor' instead of 'actress' when referring to female actors), but there is also the case of the personal choice of title being used by the person who is being reported. We can see how this might be problematic in one report by the right-wing newspaper the *Daily Mail* (5 January 2007), concerning women being obstructed in their business careers by workplace strategies to discourage maternity leave and flexible working hours. 'Bosses "block women who want a career and a family."' Within the article, two principle players are quoted: Jenny Watson 'chairman of the EOC' and Lorely Burt, who is referred to as the 'Liberal Democrat Women

Dispreferred	Preferred
Businessman	Business manager, executive, business people
Newsman	Journalist
Cameraman	Camera operator, photographer
Dustman	Refuse collector
Policeman	Police officer
Salesman	Sales staff, shop worker
Stewards/air hostess	Flight attendant
Chairman	Chairperson, chairwoman, chair
Housewife	Shopper, consumer, cook
Authoress	Author – avoid -ess where possible
Mothers	(when we mean parents)
Girls (when over 18)	Women (especially in sports reporting)
Ladies, Mrs Mopp, dolls	Women – these, and puns arising from them are not funny.
Serviceman	Armed service personnel
Male nurse/woman doctor	Nurse, doctor

FIGURE 4.3 *Adapted from NUJ guidelines.*

and Equality Spokesman'. In both cases, the women are given male-specific titles (chairman and spokesman), yet their personal preferences as shown in their respective websites was for 'chair' (in the case of Watson) and 'spokesperson' (for Burt). Thus we can see that despite NUJ guidelines and the expressed preferences of the women concerned, there is a problematic use of gender-specific language being used by the journalist. It is all the more ironic that this is a report about gender equality in the workplace.

If we return briefly to the story about Kylie Minogue attending a party, we can begin to see how different genders are reported in the media and how this goes beyond the level of lexical choice that appears to be the main concern of the NUJ's guidelines. On a basic level, the story is based around Kylie's clothes and does not mention the reason why she was attending the party. Instead, this is used as a vehicle to comment about her age and her personal life. The relationship between this and gender stereotyping is clearly articulated in Figure 3.2. It is repeat in brief in Figure 4.4.

This also links with the lexical items we looked at in Figure 4.3, where the language of public work is closely aligned to masculinity. The report about Kylie Minogue is also placing her firmly in the realms of a story based around elegance and her private life: the only quotations in this story relate to her boyfriend. Kylie's professional status is acknowledged in relation to

Men	Women
Power	Grace
Strength	Elegance
Independence	Dependence
Public life	Private life

FIGURE 4.4 *Male and female stereotypes (see also Figure 3.2).*

the release of her latest album, but this is framed within descriptions of a party-going, heterosexual lifestyle.

To illustrate this further, we will now look at the print media's representation of women during the 2010 British general election campaign. As we mentioned above, quality and popular newspapers tend to report political issues in different ways, with the popular newspapers tending towards political coverage that focuses on personal stories more than policies. The 2010 general election campaign was remarkable for the media coverage afforded to the spouses of the three main party leaders across both quality and popular newspapers, and in fact, only 10 per cent of the coverage of women in politics during this election was devoted to people other than the three wives (see Higgins and Smith, forthcoming), the majority of this appearing in the popular press. Of the three women, Sarah Brown had the highest political profile, having married the then-chancellor of the exchequer in 2000. Also, as a former PR executive, she had embraced new media such as Twitter to engage with a wider community without making overtly political statements (at the time of the election, Sarah Brown's Twitter page had more than a million followers). However, given that these three women were not actively standing for election, the overwhelming media coverage relating to them during the campaign is useful to comprehend more about the newspaper representation of gender.

Frequently, the stories reported in the print media related to comparisons between the wife of the leader of the ruling Labour Party Sarah Brown, and the wife of the leader of the opposing Conservative Party Samantha Cameron. Below is a story from the *Daily Express* (8 April 2010). This story is largely typical of the sort of coverage of Sarah Brown's and Samantha Cameron's electioneering activities that appeared in most newspapers at this time:

BATTLE OF THE FIRST WIVES: SAMANTHA CAMERON
OUT-MANOEUVRES SARAH BROWN

Daily Express, Thursday 8 April 2010

By Emily Garnham

1   GORDON BROWN attempted to win support at an east London community centre today with his devoted wife at his side – while David Cameron's other half was flying solo.

2   While Sarah Brown plays the loyal first lady, accompanying her DH (Twitter speak for darling husband) on his election campaign trail and dutifully updating her blog, Tory wife Samantha Cameron has adopted a different tactic.

3   Affectionately dubbed his 'secret weapon' the pregnant wife of Conservative leader David Cameron today visited a Christian charity for the homeless and vulnerable – without her husband in sight.

4   Wearing black jeans, Converse trainers, a grey jacket and scarf, Sam Cam blended in as she made an appearance at the Caring for Life charity in Cookridge, Leeds as her husband gave a speech in London.

5   The 38-year-old artistic director of leather goods firm Smythson was greeted by charity bosses at the working farm, located in the Liberal Democrat constituency of Leeds North West, before being shown around horticultural and woodworking projects.

6   When asked why she was visiting the charity, which provides residential housing for homeless people as well as running activities and projects, she said: 'I hope to highlight the amazing work charities like this do for some of the most vulnerable people in society, who tend to fall through the net.'

7   Speaking after her visit, the charity's founder, Peter Parkinson, described her as 'extraordinarily empathetic' and said she had a breadth of understanding of social issues.

8   He said: 'I think that probably the experience they've had as a family has meant she has an empathy for the sort of people we are caring for.'

9   'She was extraordinarily empathetic with all the people she met and also very interested.'

10 With less than a month to go before Britain goes to the polls to elect the next government, there is no doubt Mr Brown and Mr Cameron are looking to their wives to boost their profiles as dedicated family men – as well as politicians.

11 Questioned today about his wife's appearances on the Labour campaign trail, Mr Brown said: 'It's her idea, and she wants to help the campaign, and we want to work together on that.'

12 He added: 'She's the love of my life, and we work well together and we like going round the country together, and I'm looking forward to the campaign.'

13 Top of Form Bottom of Form

14 Sarah Brown's Twitter page, which has more than 1.1 million followers and gives an insight into life at No. 10 has just launched a blog on her husband's website.

15 In her first entry she writes: 'From here on in you'll get a street level view of life on the campaign trail.'

16 'I'm going to keep on doing what I've always done, which is to share details of my day and the campaigns that I'm involved in, without overwhelming you with my own political views.'

17 But with Sam Cam leading in the style stakes, and with a profile boost thanks to her recent pregnancy announcement, there's everything to play for in the battle of the first wives.

We should begin by noting that while this story concerns the wives of two of the political party leaders, and therefore deals with gender and the domestic realm, it also falls within the scope of political news. Regardless, we can see a gendered theme emerge in the naming practices, as shown in Figure 4.5.

From this list, we can see that Sarah Brown is most frequently referred to as 'wife', with one intertextual reference to her as 'first lady' (a US position that does not exist in British political culture). In a similar way, Samantha Cameron is also referred to as being affiliated with her husband. But there is greater variety in how her gender is represented elsewhere. For example, a feature of the election campaign was Samantha Cameron's pregnancy, and in 'Pregnant wife of Conservative leader' we have that adjective pre-modifying the longer noun phrase that again aligns Samantha with her husband and his political position. The name 'secret weapon' again defines Samantha in terms of her utility to her husband, as this is the inexplicit but widely known nickname he has for her. The print media's love of linguistic novelty, which at this time featured short forms of celebrities' names by merging the first

Sarah Brown	Samantha Cameron
Devoted wife	Other half
Loyal first lady	Tory wife
Wife	His secret weapon
	Pregnant wife of Conservative leader
	Sam Cam
	38-year-old artistic director of leather goods firm
	Smythson

FIGURE 4.5 *Naming practices within the article in* Daily Express, *Thursday 8 April 2010.*

syllable of first and last name (such as SuBo for Susan Boyle, a popular talent show contestant, and LiLo for actor Lindsay Lohan) is also clear here in the repeated use of Samantha Cameron's popular press nickname of Sam Cam. Only one description of Samantha does not align her with her husband or with a colloquial nickname, and that is the long noun phrase '38-year-old artistic director. . .' that highlights her highly successful professional business occupation.

If we take into account the Conservative-supporting stance of the *Daily Express*, we can also begin to detect a bias towards Samantha Cameron in the connotations behind these naming practices. For example, the adjectives used in relation to Sarah Brown – devoted, loyal – carry underlying hints of passivity, perhaps even blind devotion. This contrasts with a more independent Samantha Cameron, who is acknowledged as capable of 'flying solo' on the campaign trail as well as in her professional life.

From this list, we can see that the two women are overwhelmingly aligned with their male consorts. It is comparatively easy to think of other naming choices, such as Mrs Brown or Mrs Cameron, which even if gendered in themselves, would have been less explicit in positioning them as adjuncts to their powerful husbands. However, the gendering of these two women goes beyond simple naming practices. If we look at some of the grammatical features of the story, we can see how this extends beyond even the lexical choices outlined in the NUJ list, we looked at in Figure 4.3, and into grammatical structure.

In terms of verb structural choices, we can see the use of both active and passive voice. In English, the standard sentence structure features subject – verb – object, or SVO. The subject or active agent carries out the action on an object or affected agent. This is referred to as active voice, and these are a few examples.

Subject	Verb	object
Sarah Brown	updated	her blog
Samantha Cameron	adopted	a different tactic

Passive voice re-orders this construction with the subject or active agent following the verb, or being omitted entirely. For example:

Object	Verb	+/- subject
Her blog	was updated	by Sarah Brown
A different tactic	Was adopted	by Samantha Cameron

Passive voice can be used strategically to highlight an action rather than the actor; for example, in this story Samantha Cameron is 'shown around horticultural and woodworking projects', but it is not clear who it is that is acting as her guide. In this case, the lack of importance we should attach to the identity of the guide is made clear. Elsewhere, as mentioned above, the nickname of 'secret weapon' ascribed to Samantha Cameron is rendered in passive voice ('affectionately dubbed' is left without an agent), which thereby backgrounds the part David Cameron has had in making his wife more marketable. However, if we look more closely at the verbs used in the story, we can see that there is a deeper reading available, such that it becomes clear that it is not just the case that active and passive voice can reveal something about how gender is represented.

Drawing on M. A. K. Halliday's function grammar, we can divide verbs into the broad categories of actional and relational, before subdividing them further (see Figure 4.6).

As the names suggests, actional verbs carry with them some sort of physical action. Verbs which grammatically carry out an action on another agent/object are called 'transactive' verbs. In the example above, Sarah is carrying out an action that is affecting her husband. However, grammatically, these actional verbs do not all necessarily carry an action on another object/agent. Such verbs are referred to as being 'non-transactive', and an example of such a verb is given above in the sentence 'Samantha was flying solo'. Here, the action attached to Samantha is offered as having no effect on anyone or anything else. There is a simple test to find out whether an actional verb is transactive or non-transactive: if the sentence can be made passive, then it is a transactive verb. In the example above, the passive voice construction of the transactive verb would be 'Her husband was accompanied (by Sarah)'. This may sound clumsy, but still makes grammatical sense. On the other hand, the non-transactive utterance 'Samantha was flying solo' cannot be made sense of in passive voice ('solo was being flown by Samantha').

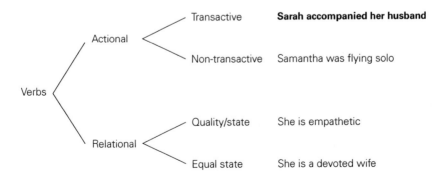

FIGURE 4.6 *Diagram of actional/relational verbs.*

The so-called relational verbs are verbs which do not carry an action with them, but instead offer information about the quality or state of the active agent, or else offer details of equal state. These verb constructions cannot be made passive.

From this, we can begin to see that non-transactive verbs and both sorts of relational verbs carry minimal effect with them: they are only affecting the person who is carrying out the action. We can see how this relates to representations of women in the media if we return to the *Daily Express* story about Sarah Brown and Samantha Cameron. As noted above, much of the story is written in active voice with strategic use of passive voice. However, if we look at the verbs in more detail, then we can see how something more complicated is going on.

Sarah Brown, in the second paragraph, is represented using transactive verbs in active voice. As noted earlier, these verbs work to place her in a supporting role of obedient wife. Samantha Cameron, by contrast, is represented in the third paragraph with the transactive verb 'visit', but this is heavily pre-modified (as we noted earlier) by the description of her that links her with her husband and maternity. In the fourth paragraph another transactive verb choice relates to her clothes (describing what she is wearing in some detail). The only other transactive verb choice relating to her comes in the final paragraph, where it again relates to her clothing, where she is described as 'leading in the style stakes'.

Elsewhere, both Samantha and Sarah are linked with the transactive verb construction of 'saying' or 'writing', and this is followed by direct quotations. The quotations themselves, if we look at them closely, are vacuous and are repeated and expanded on by male participants (the charity manager, in Samantha Cameron's case, and Gordon Brown in Sarah's). In fact, Sarah Brown is robbed of active agency in paragraph 13, where technology in the form of her Twitter page is the active agent in providing information to the public (even then, this is linked to 'her husband' through a reference to Gordon's website).

This begins to look more remarkable when we contrast the expression of the activities of the women with that of the men in the same article. When it comes to the men, we can see power and active agency. For example, in the first paragraph, Gordon Brown is 'attempting to win support' and in the fourth paragraph David Cameron is 'giving a speech in London'. In both cases, these are public actions that carry real power and authority. Both leaders are then collocated in the tenth paragraph where they are described as 'looking to their wives to boost their profiles as dedicated family men'. So here we find, explicitly, the strategic use of the women in the public sphere to shed light on their lives beyond the public sphere.

Overall, if we look at how these women are framed, we find that they are supportive in both the grammatical sense and also in the pragmatic sense. The attention to the visual appearance of the leaders' wives in newspaper reporting of the election campaign, as seen here in the reference to Samantha Cameron's outfit, can be related to the grace and elegance expected of women in the stereotypes outlined above. This representation of the wives of the political party leaders, with an emphasis on domesticity and passivity aligned with visual appearance, can also be seen in the story about Kylie Minogue that we looked at earlier.

Conclusion

In looking at the language of newspaper journalism, we have examined the structures and lexical choices of headlines and news stories. We have suggested that one of the key considerations in looking at newspaper discourse in a market such as Britain is the difference between popular and quality newspapers. But we have also argued that discourses of gender and identity are important in understanding newspapers, often bound up with parallel discourses of celebrity and popular culture. These representations, we have found, are apparent both in lexical choices over naming and describing participants in a story, as well as the grammatical structures within which their activities are described.

5

Sports journalism

Introduction

In this chapter we are going to look at the particular language of sports journalism. This type of journalism occupies a difficult and sometimes contentious place in the news industry. In an article arguing for its importance, David Rowe (2007: 386) reflects regretfully on its characterization as the 'toy department' of the newsroom: where a male-dominated culture is free to indulge in pastimes, confecting controversy from frivolity. In fact, Rowe argues that in terms of its capacity to deal with social and political issues and the degree of professionalism required, sports journalism out-performs many of the more outwardly 'serious' genres.

In terms of its expressive obligations and potential as well, this chapter will show there is much to be gained from the study of sports journalism. We will look at the particular forms of linguistic performance in live commentary, separating out the component types of speech in live commentary and showing how these types foster hierarchies both in the expression and organization of the commentary. We will also look at the capacity of sports journalism to promote formations of national identity. Looking at the example of England vs. Germany, we will show how popular-historical discourses unite to motivate a sense of national togetherness, against an excluded and marginalized 'other'. As we will see throughout this chapter, sports journalism expresses far more than our relationship with sport.

Sports commentary

To begin with, we are going to look at 'live' commentary on sports events. Live commentary has a number of exceptional qualities. First, more than any other form of journalistic comments and description, it deals with what Stephanie Marriott (2007: 76) describes as the '*now*-moment in which stuff is happening'. It therefore demands a reflexivity and responsiveness unusual even for an industry fixated with timeliness. Second, live commentary uses this lexicon of responsiveness to generate excitement in the audience; often by 'communicating a sense of high-drama in the events of screen [or on radio or webcast]' (Rowe, 2004: 118). Garry Whannel (1992: 26) describes this as 'on the one hand the impulse to describe the scene, give the audience an accurate picture, and on the other the impulse to get people involved, keep up the interest, add suspense, shape the material and highlight the action'. It is this pressure to avoid a deadening silence, according to Rowe (2004: 119), that gives rise to so many of the apparent 'inanities and infelicities' that are routinely used to characterize sports commentary and subject it to occasional ridicule.

However, we will see that commentary is far more organized and open to analysis than its everyday-criticism within the industry and among sports aficionados would have us believe. Typically, commentary has a structure and contains linguistic features that can be applied across the treatment of different sports. We have mentioned other books that have looked at the use of 'liveness' in sports commentary (Marriott, 2007) and the use of direct address (Whannel, 1992). We will follow Judy Delin's linguistic exploration of sports commentary, eventually linking this to how community is created, as we looked at in Chapters 3 and 4.

Looking at the structure of the commentary, we can see that there are four main types of utterances.

1 *Narration*: time-critical description of what is happening play-by-play.

2 *Evaluating*: giving opinions about play, players, teams, referee decisions, etc.

3 *Elaborating*: providing background information about team and player records, the ground, the crowd; speculating on motives and thoughts of players.

4 *Summarizing*: giving occasional overviews of play and results thus far.
   (Delin, 2000: 46)

If we are to assume that the main purpose of live commentary is to describe what is happening, then narration is the best form of utterance to accomplish this. The live-ness of a sporting event is encompassed in narration through a description of what is going on at the time of play. However, the three other main types of utterances tend to be deployed during quieter periods of an on-going event, or when there has been a particularly noteworthy occurrence on the pitch that requires more than a basic, time-critical description. These types of utterances tend to be more explicitly subjective, often drawing the reputation and expertise of the commentator, as suggested by their labels — evaluative, elaborative or summative.

Commentary: Managing styles

By looking in some detail at the different utterance types in a football commentary, we can see how there are actually two different roles ascribed to the two commentators, but that switching between styles is far more complex and responsive than these roles suggest. The transcript here is from the Germany–England match at Bloemfontein in the 2010 World Cup finals, and to start with we are going to look in some detail at a stretch of commentary taken from early in the game before either team had scored, also bringing in examples from a part of the match where the commentators are discussing a disallowed goal. The match was broadcast live on BBC1 on Sunday, 27 June 2010, and we are going to be looking at the commentary team of Guy Mowbray, who is a long-standing professional sports journalist working for the BBC, and retired professional footballer Mark Lawrenson. This arrangement has become customary for live sporting events in British broadcasting: to have two members of the 'commentary team', one of whom is often a former or current professional in the relevant sport.

In an embodiment of Delin's (2000: 46) categorization, only one of the commentators is called upon to narrate, while the second commentator is only called upon to evaluate during slower parts of the game, and provide occasional elaborative and summative utterances. So, the professional journalist, here Guy Mowbray, exclusively provides the narration, while the retired footballer, Mark Lawrenson, provides additional information which can draw on his experiences as a player at the highest level. Important too for the relationship between the commentators and the event, the visual images made available to the viewer are not under the control of the BBC, but are shot by FIFA-nominated camera operators and directors.

In Figure 5.1, we can see all four utterance types, as set out earlier (pauses are indicated by bracketed stops and then by numbers of seconds).

We can immediately see the need to switch between types. Mowbray's first utterance on line 1 ('Rooney (4) ups it to Terry') is an example of narration, describing the live action. However, his next utterance on that line is evaluative, as he speculates on whether the recipient of the pass welcomed the move ('I'm not sure he quite wanted that'). Mowbray then reverts to narrative in line two ('Ashley Cole (3) Vincent Ozil') before switching to elaboration, where he gives us more information about the German player (German born (.) Turkish

Mowbray	Rooney (4) ups it to Terry (.) I'm not sure he quite wanted	1
	that (2) Ashley Cole (3) Vincent Ozil (.) German born (.)	2
	Turkish father (.) is a very clever footballer (.) only twenty	3
	one	4
		5
Lawrenson	There's a few Polish born as well isn't there in this team	6
		7
Mowbray	Yeh it really is the the rainbow nation this Germany squad	8
	(4) like for us with South Africans on the cricket field I	9
	suppose (4) here's Defoe (.) now Glen Johnson (4) Milner	10
	(4) in towards Defoe (.) it was a good header from	11
	Mertesacker (.) Defoe was trying to let it run for Rooney	12
		13
Lawrenson	The good thing as well is that Boateng really just let Milner	14
	cross it	

FIGURE 5.1 *Commentary on 2010 World Cup Finals, BBC1, Sunday, 27 June 2010, extract 1.*

father'), before immediately switching again to evaluation to offer his opinion that Ozil is a 'very clever footballer'. Lawrenson's interjection on line 6 is elaborative ('there's a few Polish born as well'), although it is framed as a question through the tag 'isn't there', thereby inviting Mowbray to respond with a further elaborative utterance on line 8. There is then a four-second gap in the commentary on line 8 before Mowbray continues with the narrative utterance describing the game on lines 10–12, before then offering evaluation on lines 11–12. Lawrenson then comes in on line 14 with a summary of what has happened in the last few minutes on the pitch.

There are also indicators of the relative spontaneity that is necessary to live commentary. At this point, we can see Mowbray having to repair what may be unkindly interpreted as a discriminatory utterance that has been collaborated on by the two commentators in lines 2–6, where the ethnic origins of several of the German squad has been discussed, and where Mowbray begins to ameliorate possible misreadings by referring to the German team as a 'rainbow nation' (lines 8). After his initial intervention and four-second pause, Mowbray then draws on a collective knowledge of the ethnicity of the English cricket team, linking the commentary with wider debates about the inclusion of players who are not born in England in the team. Hinting at a pattern we will return to later in the chapter, there is a clear distinction between 'us' (the English, to whom the analogy applies) and the interloping 'them' (those South Africans included in the England team).

What remains as the most rigid component of the relationship between style and commentator is that narration is the exclusive preserve of the professional journalist in the commentary team. Moreover, Delin suggests, other than the occasion lapse or breakdown of roles, the exclusivity of the 'main' commentator in describing the action is common to live commentary across sports.

Commentary: Managing speakers

In circumstances where there are two people commenting on a game, we need to look at how speaker change is managed. Often this is simply by switching from one type of utterance to another, marked by a gap of a few seconds, as we have seen in Figure 5.1. However, if we go back to turn-taking, as we looked at in Chapter 2, we can see how the normal rules of successful speaker management apply (see Graddol et al., 1999: 162). While there are discrete activities, usually two or more of these turn-taking cues occur at the same time.

- *Explicit nomination*: speaker A can name speaker B explicitly, giving them an explicit cue.
- *Pause*: a gap allowing other speakers to come in and speak.
- *Syntactic completion*: there is a clear end to the utterance indicated by grammatical structure.
- *Intonation*: falling intonation, or rising for a question, may indicate turn completion.

In addition, direction of gaze or the exchange of looks may also play a role, although even in television commentary where the cameras focus on the sporting action, the analyst is in no position to gauge the role of the gaze between the interactants (even though studio-based panel discussions can offer such an opportunity).

It is remarkable that in sports commentary there is very little overlap between speakers. Overlaps do tend to occur at periods of heightened excitement but they are usually very brief. Figure 5.2 shows the overlap which occurs in the commentary following England's disallowed goal, and so is a period of confusion.

The overlap on line 4 by Lawrenson shows him attempting to add to his indignant evaluation of a perceived lack of assiduousness on the part of the governing body of world football, FIFA, in particular the president Sepp Blatter. Lawrenson's passionate disgust at the inaction of this individual overrides the conventions of sports commentary, and when Mowbray attempts to change the evaluation to a closer focus on the England team on line 4, after a

Lawrenson	What is it FIFA don't want (1) technology (.) thanks very much Sepp Blatter (4)	1 2 3
Mowbray	England could /lose this	4 5
Lawrenson	/Well I hope he's here and he's squirming in his seat by the way	6 7

FIGURE 5.2 *Commentary on 2010 World Cup Finals, BBC1, Sunday, 27 June 2010, extract 2.*

four-second pause Lawrenson continues his diatribe on Blatter through lines 6 and 7. Mowbray concedes the floor to Lawrenson by not elaborating on his speculative evaluation ('England could lose this'), perhaps explained in this particular case by Mowbray's role as journalist discouraging him from giving voice to his personal frustration. Mowbray therefore steps back and allows former-footballer Lawrenson to continue to express his annoyance as an elaborating utterance.

It is important to note that these cues are *opportunities* for the other commentator to take the floor rather than commands or obligations for them to do so. Most of the time, speaker change occurs without a discernable gap where there is a collaborative evaluative or elaborative utterance. But elsewhere, there are utterances which follow longer gaps of several seconds, which are not always taken as potential opportunities for change of turn. Indeed, within this television commentary, we can see many examples of lengthy pauses where there is no speaker change. For example, in Figure 5.3 we can see Mowbray commenting on an unsuccessful appeal against an off-side decision (line 1), before resuming narration (lines 1–7) further evaluation (lines 7–11).

Whether or not a cue to take the floor is accepted depends largely on the development of the dialogue between the commentators, and whether disagreements have arisen. Mowbray's syntactic completion of his elaborative utterance on line 11 is not followed by a noticeable gap, but Lawrenson picks up on this elaborative utterance and offers his own elaboration to balance out the implied assertion that there is more pressure on the German players to win, owing to their long record of World Cup success. In keeping with the 'politeness' strategies outlined by Brown and Levinson (1987), his is turned into a question through the use of the tag 'isn't it' (line 13), followed by a short gap, which is not taken up by Mowbray, so occasioning further elaboration by Lawrenson. This embellishment is continued after a gap of four seconds, when Mowbray takes the floor to imply that there has to be one winner (something viewers would be aware of, given the match is taking place in

Mowbray	His claim was the biggest thing (.) passed back [shots of	1
	German corner] Schweinsteiger (.) out comes James (.)	2
	that's a good solid catch (5) gone for the punt (.) Friedrich's	3
	touch (.) picked out by Baoteng (.) there's Schweinsteiger	4
	(.) finds Muller (2) just swapping sides for a moment (3)	5
	Schweinsteiger plays it against Johnson to get Germany	6
	the throw-in (6) young or not (.) there's arguably just as	7
	much pressure on this German team as the er more	8
	experienced England players (.) they've only once failed	9
	to reach the last eight of a World Cup and that was in	10
	nineteen thirty eight	11
		12
Lawrenson	I think it's the same for both isn't it (.) we expect England	13
	to win and the Germans expect their team to win (4)	14
		15
Mowbray	Can't both be happy at the end of the day (2)	16
		17
Lawrenson	[laughing] Right (4)	18
		19
Mowbray	This is going through and Friedrich and Neuer will be happy	20
	for it to do so (4)	

FIGURE 5.3 *Commentary on 2010 World Cup Finals, BBC1, Sunday, 27 June 2010, extract 3.*

the knock-out stages of the tournament), by noting that one team/nation will be disappointed. Another gap of two seconds is needed before Lawrenson concurs, then there is silence of four seconds before Mowbray resumes the narration of events on the pitch. Here, then, we can see the commentators cooperatively filling the gap in the narration during a 'quiet' period of play, although it is apparent that cues are not always taken up, and other strategies can be employed to keep the commentary going.

Hierarchies of utterance and commentator

Overall, as Delin points out, the main purpose of sports commentary is narration – events as they unfold are being described to viewers/listeners. On this basis, narration takes priority over other types of utterance. Occasionally, this ranking is manifest in the professional journalist commentator having warrant to resume narration if something remarkable happens on the pitch whilst the pundit commentator is evaluating, elaborating or summarizing. More frequently, though, this precedence of narration is clear from the dis-fluencies in the talk, where a contribution by the pundit is not enjoined by the journalist commentator, who instead resumes narration of events on the pitch. Figure 5.4 presents a brief example.

Contrary to norms of politeness, we can see that Lawrenson's summary of a previous match is not continued by Mowbray, who instead resumes the narration of the on-pitch action, choosing not to develop the topic of England's previous strategies further at this point.

However, as we can also see from this interruption, such hierarchies of prominence apply to the commentators as well as the utterance. While the use of names to manage turn-taking is quite rare, in Figure 5.5 we find an example when Mowbray calls on Lawrenson to offer his opinion as former player of the likely state of mind of the England players following a disallowed goal.

Delin's analysis of football commentary points to unequal power relations between the two commentators, in an arrangement where the professional journalist/commentator occupies a position of dominance. One sign of this supremacy that Delin highlights is the use of nomination by the professional journalist towards the co-commentator, where they call upon them by name to speak. More common than this, however, are a cooperative and complex set of arrangements, involving, although as we have seen, the unequal distribution of types of utterance, in a way that favours the commentator.

There are, however, occasional elements of narration from the former player that we can point to. The commentary in Figure 5.6 came soon after England's disallowed goal and follows a heated discussion on the use of goal-line technology.

Lawrenson	It was one of the things about Slovenia the other night was	1
	that England played the diagonal ball very well (2)	2
		3
Mowbray	It's Boateng's throw (3) Terry (6) Rooney didn't know where	4
	the ball was (3) then Johnson (3) Germany's goal kick (8)	5

FIGURE 5.4 *Commentary on 2010 World Cup Finals, BBC1, Sunday, 27 June 2010, extract 4.*

Mowbray	It's pay-back for the Germans (5) well they've got to use	1
	that Mark haven't they?	2
		3
Lawrenson	Yes (.) most definitely (6)	4

FIGURE 5.5 *Commentary on 2010 World Cup Finals, BBC1, Sunday, 27 June 2010, extract 5.*

| Mowbray | Well I don't care what vantage point you've got inside this stadium (1) but you could see that (4) it's out (.) and it's a Germany throw (5) | Ball crossed out for German throw. | 1 2 3 4 5 |
| Lawrenson | Well the crowd are giving the referee abuse but (1) if you don't see it (.) you can't give it (5) she's telling him (3) | Shots of throw-in with England supporters clearly shouting at referee behind player | 6 7 8 9 10 |

FIGURE 5.6 *Commentary on 2010 World Cup Finals, BBC1, Sunday, 27 June 2010, extract 6.*

Here, we can see Mowbray continuing an elaboration on the referee failing to see the ball cross the line for a goal, before returning to narration on line 4 to resume his live commentary of events on the pitch. However the former player Lawrenson sees activities off the pitch that deserve remark: an England fan is seen gesticulating behind the German player about to take the throw-in. Although play is not actually taking place at this time, Lawrenson's comment on line 10 – 'she's telling him' – could be regarded as being a narrative utterance. However, as soon as play resumes, Mowbray immediately positions himself at the centre of the narrative frame.

This also calls our attention to the role of visual images on screen. On the one hand, commentary often performs a deictic function; 'pointing' to something or someone within the visual field (of the fan, 'she's telling him'). Also, the visual images mean that the lengthy gaps in the commentary do not figure as 'dead air', as the silences allow that the viewers can see for themselves that there may be a lull in the action on the pitch, without having this rendered as an explicit part of the narration (such as retrieving the ball or organizing players for 'set pieces' such as corners, throw-ins and free kicks). In the case of radio sports commentary, the 'dead ball' time is usually filled with evaluative, elaborative or summarizing utterances, or, famously in cricket commentary, with talk on other matters altogether.

Overall, the commentary arrangement is therefore a collaborative one, with recognized power relations in place, mainly through the convention of priority being given to narrative utterances, and these being uttered only by the professional journalist commentator. This is an example of what Sacks (1992) suggests as the ability of speakers to identify turn types (here, based on the four main types of utterances) and so understand how turn-taking can be managed when there is the possibility of interruption and overlap.

Commentary and shared emotions

We have spoken about cooperation between the commentators. Commentators also act in accord by sharing humorous exchanges, engaging in *banter*. An example of this is to be found in Figure 5.3, lines 13–18, beginning with Lawrenson's question to Mowbray 'I think it's the same for both isn't it' and then Lawrenson laughing at Mowbray's reply. This display of shared humour in their commentary suggests to the overhearing audience that they are in the company of people who are not only knowledgeable about the sport, but are of a friendly and light-hearted disposition (we also saw this in men's magazines, where humour is used as a form of positive politeness).

These performances of shared emotion also extend the relationship of the commentators to the teams and to the community they shared with viewers. The dialogue between the two commentators allows the overhearing audience access to an informed discussion involving regular participants who are assuming shared knowledge of the teams and previous matches. This sense of community is also clear through an expression of shared incredulity following England's disallowed goal (see Figure 5.7).

Here, the turn-taking is clearly identified by the questions posed by Lawrenson (lines 1 and 7), and amounts to an exchange of expressions of disbelief. These are underpinned by a shared sense of injustice that is directed at the governing body of world football and its decision not to use the sort of technology that the commentators are certain would have allowed the England goal to stand ('FIFA issued their edict a couple of months ago (1) end of debate (2) no goal-line technology'). Thus the criticisms are directed not at the referee (Lawrenson spends quite some time defending the referee who had not been placed to actually see the ball cross the line), but rather the alleged incompetence and money-grabbing in FIFA.

Lawrenson	Everyone is in a state of shock aren't they	1
		2
Mowbray	Well it's quite incredible (.) we had all the talk in the build-up to	3
	the World Cup (.) FIFA issued their edict a couple of months ago	4
	(1) end of debate (2) no goal-line technology (3)	5
		6
Lawrenson	What's the profit they'll make from this World Cup? (2)	7
		8
Mowbray	A frightening amount (4) the linesman from Uruguay not Russia	9
	(5)	

FIGURE 5.7 *Commentary on 2010 World Cup Finals, BBC1, Sunday, 27 June 2010, extract 7.*

The community here is forged through knowledge as well as shared indignation: in particular, the reference on line 9 to the linesman being 'from Uruguay not Russia'. To out-group members, this might appear to be a confusing reference that has little apparent relevance to the game or the discussion at this point. However, in-group England football fans would be familiar with the historical reference of the 'Russian Linesman' as alluding to linesman Tofik Bakhramov, who confirmed to the referee in the 1966 World Cup Final that the controversial Geoff Hurst goal in extra time had crossed the line. This shared knowledge on the circumstances in 1966 emerges again in Mowbray's comment in Figure 5.5 that the incident under discussion is 'pay-back for the Germans'. We will return shortly to the sports discourses that give rise to such references, as they are central to the sense of community that sports journalism is complicit in creating.

Micro-linguistic features

From the above, it will now be clear that the micro-linguistic features of commentary also contribute to the differences between types of utterance, and we can add a little to this here. We have seen that one of the main functions of narration is to describe who is in control of play. If we look again at the transcripts that feature narration, we can see there are some specific linguistic features that enable us to recognize this. For one, narration is constrained by time, and lengthy pauses indicate either a lull in play or that a particular player has control of the ball. For example, in Figure 5.3, we can tell from the lengthy pauses in Mowbray's narration that the ball is in play but possession has not changed, with the longest pause of five seconds indicating that the ball is in the air after the England keeper, David James, has kicked it back down the pitch (referred to here by the colloquial footballing register as 'gone for the punt' (Figure 5.3, line 3).

Another feature of the narration is its employment of short noun phrases, primarily the players' names, together with the minimal use of verbs. This is a characteristic quality of sports commentary and calls upon the radio listeners in particular to have a reasonable grasp of the names of the relevant players to at least understand which team has possession. In Figure 5.3, for example, the kick by James ends up with Friedrich, and so the viewer has to establish for themselves that possession has changed from England to Germany.

The verb tense in the narration also plays an important role. As this is 'time-critical commentary' (Delin, 2000: 46), it is largely given in present tense. In Delin's discussion of sports commentary (47), she suggested that the verbs used in narration are not finite (i.e. they do not carry tense), but we can see from the examples here that this is not exclusively the case. There is an example of a non-finite verb on line 5, where two of the German players are described as 'swapping sides', but other verb choices are finite (Figure 3, line 5: 'finds Muller'; line 6: 'plays it against Johnson'). We can also see that there is a limited use of past tense in the narration, where Mowbray comments on an immediately previous action that has appeared on screen (e.g. Figure 5.3: line 1, 'passed back'; line 3 'gone for the punt'). However, the overall impression that remains is the sense of liveness.

Sports journalism and national identity

Having started thinking about sports journalism and communal belonging, this section explores how national identity is constructed in sports reporting, and how this is closely aligned with militaristic discourses (see Blain, Boyle and O'Donnell, 1993; Blain and O'Donnell, 1998). During the Euro '96 football tournament, several studies of newspaper coverage across Europe found that sporting success or failure tended to be reported in terms of contemporary economic and political references (see Blain and O'Donnell, 1998; Maguire, Poulton and Possamai, 1999; Garland and Rowe, 1999). Moreover, in the case of British media reporting of sport, it has widely been observed that success or failure symbolizes the success or failure of the nation. It is suggested that this stems from a post-imperialistic sense of loss, where as Maguire et al. (1998, 1999) argue, there is a 'wilful nostalgia', involving a persistent reference to a supposed glorious military and imperial past. This can be seen most clearly in the metaphors that are employed by journalists when reporting sporting events and help to construct a sense of national unity.

Sport, particularly that which features 'national' teams, can be used to construct what Benedict Anderson (2006) refers to as an 'imagined community'. The media's role in constructing such a community is vital for the unification of the country. As Stuart Hall has argued:

> National cultures are composed not only of cultural institutions, but of symbols and representations. A national culture is a discourse – a way of constructing meanings which influences and organises both our actions and our conception of ourselves [. . .] National cultures construct identities by producing meanings about 'the nation' with which we can identify; these are contained in the stories which are told about it, memories which connect its present with its past, and images which are constructed of it. (1992: 292–293)

Since the 1996 European Championships in football, the English national team has been closely associated with the red and white flag of St George. This symbol of Englishness has spread to other sports where 'England' is playing, and crops up in the visual imagery we find appearing in the media when reporting such events. As a visual symbol, it binds sports and nation and thus acts as a semiotic code for unity and common interest. As Martin Conboy (2006) has observed of tabloid newspapers in particular, the overt emphasis on the home nation is useful for the popular newspapers:

> It is only because of the constant presence of such an iconography and symbolism that the tabloids can move into a more explicit mode on set occasions, in full confidence that they are articulating sentiments which are familiar to their readers. (2006: 53)

Such an emphasis on the nation is also present in the lexicon used in sports journalism; there are frequent references to '1966': the year in which the English football team won the World Cup. This date then becomes a semiotic code for a golden past and can be used in reference to other sports where the 'spirit of '66' is evoked as the pinnacle of British sporting achievement. Also, in keeping with what Michael Billig (1995) describes as a 'banal', everyday sense of national belonging, news is composed around a mood of inclusiveness and mutuality, driven by the assumption that all are committed to the nation's success.

This retrospective view of a national narrative is not restricted to references to a 'golden age' of sporting glory. Outside of sporting achievement, the language of war is drawn upon to 'give meaning' to the event. As Anthony Smith (1998: 66) has observed, historical referents such as war are vital to the continuing discursive formation of the nation. This can be entwined visually with the iconic Alfred Leet recruitment poster from the First World War, in which Kitchener is seen to interpolate the passerby through his extended pointing finger and the phrase 'Your country needs YOU'. Pastiches of this image are a common staple of newspaper front pages, usually reproduced against the background of the flag of St George, repeating the phrase and even the hand-drawn Edwardian font, but replacing the face of Kitchener with that of a leading England football player. More recently, this has been re-written to pun on the nickname of the England footballer Wayne Rooney, in 'Your country needs ROO'.

Other popular metaphors are explicitly linked to the Second Word War. References to the 'Battle of Britain', somewhat perversely, present a cliché when English and Scottish teams play against each other. When the English team is under pressure in high-profile tournaments, moreover, they are encouraged to draw on the 'Blitz spirit'. Hall (1992) has referred to how in national identity 'the confusion and disasters of history are rendered intelligible', converting disarray into 'community' (such as the Blitz) and 'disasters into triumphs' (such as Dunkirk). This can be clearly seen in the way in which sports reporting draws on these metaphors of war to produce a collected heritage and desire to see that heritage realized.

An historical citation with an even greater vintage is frequently called upon at the start of international tournaments in which an English team is taking part. This slogan – 'England Expects' – is conventionally accompanied by an image depicting the relevant 'English' players standing to attention in their team colours. The phrase is the commonly shortened form of the signal 'England expects that every man will do his duty', sent by Admiral Nelson to the British fleet immediately before the Battle of Trafalgar in 1805. This was a battle subsequently won by Nelson's ships, through which they were able to wrest control of the sea from the French navy. This phrase is so closely aligned to sport, and national pride in football in particular, that James Corbett's history of the English national football team could simply be titled 'England Expects' (2010).

These allusions to the slogans and clichés of past wars serve to collocate sport with militarism, part of a process that Ernest Gellner (1983) refers to as 'the unifying impulse' that drives the sentiments of national identity. Any such compulsion is aligned with Hall's description of the fostering of a common membership of the 'family of the nation' (1992: 297). In sports reporting, and in line with Billig's (1995) notion of 'banal' nationalism, this can be seen through the assumption that the audience will participate in a shared assumption that the national team represents the people within the country. For an example of this, we can look at an editorial that appeared in the *News of the World* following the English ruby team's victory in the rugby World Cup in 2003:

> We do not win much, we English, but when we do we appreciate that if it is to burn in the memory and live forever, it is best made when the stakes are highest and the sensory over-load almost too much to bear. One such triumph came in Sydney's Olympic Stadium yesterday. Another came in Wembley in '66. And when Steve Redgrave won a fifth gold by fractions of a second we felt the same. (23 November 2003)

If we look at the assumptions of shared knowledge, we can see that there are references to events that are not explained fully in this text as it is taken for granted that the reader will have access to the relevant story and so not require further elaboration. Invoked here is what Paul Simpson (1993: 125) describes as a 'logical presupposition', where the editorial includes an entailment upon which the truth-value of the sentence rests. Specifically, the clause 'but when we do' assumes that a 'win' has now taken place. Indeed, the recency of the World Cup victory allows the knowing reference to 'one such triumph'. In line with the historical discourses described above, this is juxtaposed with the well-worn reference to the England football World Cup victory, here abbreviated by reference to the venue and year ('Wembley in '66'). The third 'triumph' relates to the Olympic success of rower Steve Redgrave, who had won a fifth gold medal at the 2000 Sydney Olympics, competing for Great Britain.

If we look at the pronouns in this short editorial, we can see how there is a further emphasis on shared sense of community. In the first sentence, the collective pronoun 'we' creates an explicitly 'English' community ('we do not win much, we English'), but this is the English nation rather than the sports team. While the actual act of winning is the responsibility of the sports players, the triumph is neatly glossed as being that of the nation by the joining of the players and spectators in the pronoun itself. Any distinction in the form of a reader who might not be English, or even interested in the achievements of a rugby team is disregarded by a nationalist discourse that collapses differences in class, gender, race and political ideology, and contains all within the same great national family.

The national media often symbolically conveys the extent of unity by broadcasting footage of empty streets and shopping centres during major sporting events. We can see this from the next report, published during the 2010 World Cup, when the *Daily Star* describes a sense of national anxiety and jubilation in its report of the England–Slovenia match:

1   England's army of nervous fans finally had something to celebrate last night after the 1–0 victory that kept our World Cup dreams alive.

2   The whole country sprung back to life at 4.48 p.m. after our nail-biting 1–0 win over minnows Slovenia in Port Elizabeth [. . .]

3   Earlier in the day England had ground to a halt, with major roads deserted and normally busy shopping centres empty.

4   Many schools finished lessons early so pupils and teachers could get home to watch the crucial match.

5   Other head teachers and business bosses across the country made special arrangements to enable fans to down tools and watch the game.

6   Sun-drenched music fans gathering for this weekend's Galstonbury rock festival even watched the drama unfold on a big screen.

7   Workers who did stay at their desks in the City of London managed to sneak a peak at the game on their computer screens, normally used for trading stocks and shares.

(*Daily Star*, 24 June 2010)

Even beyond the use of collective inclusive pronouns (e.g., paragraph 1: 'our World Cup hopes'; paragraph 2: 'our nail-biting 1–0 win'), this piece describes a sense of national unity that transcends age and social class. From school children to youthful music fans, shoppers to city workers: the presumed demographic of supporters glosses over the accompanying pictures of predominantly white men. However, as expressed through the language of the report, the 'whole country' has been watching the match, a point emphasized in paragraph 2 by the precision of the time at which the match ended this 'whole country sprung back to life'. All of this serves to reinforce the idea of an imagined community of millions which, Eric Hobsbawm (1990: 43) wryly notes, 'seems more real as a team of eleven named people'.

Sporting nationalism: Inclusion and exclusion

Having seen how the media can create a sense of national unity in sports reporting, we will now turn to how the linguistic devices that were used to create this same sense of unity can be employed to create a sense of distinction between those within and those outside of the national fold: 'us' and 'them'. To do this, we can continue with our discussion of the reporting of the 2010 World Cup in South Africa, looking in more detail at how national identity is being collocated with militarism as it coincided with the seventieth anniversary of the Second World War's 'Battle of Britain'.

In the event, the 2010 World Cup saw the England football team perform significantly below expectations. However, the lacklustre progression from the group stages of the tournament set England up for a game against Germany, and a number of the newspapers could not resist drawing on old clichés. For example, the *Daily Star's* front page headline on 24 June was the rhythmical: 'Job done . . . now for the Hun', and inside the headline 'Now bring on the Krauts'. These colloquial and broadly seen as offensive terms used by the *Daily Star* to describe the German team are now sparingly used, even by other red-top tabloids. For their part, the *Sun* settled for the homophonic pun 'Herr we go again'. In contrast to the negative portrayal of the Germans, the England team were referred to as 'lions', with associated verbs of 'roaring' and 'mauling rivals'. 'Three Lions' is the label frequently used to denote the England football team by the tabloid press, and refers to the crest on the official team badge.

However, as we saw above in the analysis of sports commentary, the England team were defeated by Germany in the next match. However, as the 2010 tournament progressed, the 'lions' tag came to be recast by journalists in a disparaging way. To take one example, Richard Littlejohn's column in the *Daily Mail* (28 June) ran with the headline 'Three Lions? More like the cowardly lion from the Wizard of Oz'. Littlejohn goes on to draw more deeply on English national identity, making intertextual links with Churchill's wartime speeches to cast the England team in an unfavourable light: 'Thank Heaven The Few didn't defend as badly as England's footballers in Bloemfontein yesterday afternoon, otherwise we'd all be speaking German.' This hyperbolic framing of the England football players as being comparable with 'The Few' is a direct allusion to Churchill's famous rallying speech during the Battle of Britain in 1940, including the famous line 'Never in the field of human conflict was so much owed by so many to so few'. In popular British culture, The Few has therefore come to refer to the RAF pilots that fought during the Battle of Britain in the summer of 1940, and here offers an easy comparison between defence against German attack in warfare and defence against the skill and endeavour of the German football team. The *Daily Mail* paraphrased this quotation from Littlejohn's column on the front page of their paper, accompanied by a picture of a despairing Wayne Rooney.

While clichéd, such historical references are not isolated. This intertextual reference to this particular speech of Churchill's occurred earlier in the same campaign, when the *Sun* paraphrased it as the headline on their back page following England's 0–0 draw with Algeria: 'never in the field of conflict has so little been offered by so few to so many . . . (with apologies to Winston Churchill)' (*Sun*, 19 June 2010). In this case, the subversion of 'little' for 'much' creates the desired sense of dark irony. The subsequent report makes the link with Churchill and military conflict even clearer, stating that 'on the day they were expected to produce their "finest hour" to mark the 70th anniversary of Winston Churchill's famous wartime speech, the Three Lions whimpered rather than roared'. Of course, there is no real attention to historical accuracy required here: 'The Few' speech was actually made by Churchill in parliament on 20 August 1940, while the speech in which Churchill talks of the 'Finest Hour' was made on 18 June 1940. So it would appear that the *Sun* has conflated the two speeches for dramatic effect.

In this way, the England football team was 'othered' through unfavourable references to a golden past, specifically a military past. In many forums, including popular journalism, the historical relationship with Germany in particular has become part of Britain's national sense of itself. The lesson here is that the use of linguistic and visual symbols that speak of this history should be situated within a journalistic context of shared-knowledge and humour.

However we should also be alert to how these activities of 'othering' are directed elsewhere, often using less specific symbolism and drawing upon deeper perceptions. The 2010 World Cup was notable for it being the first time the tournament had been held in Africa. Much of the media coverage explored the wider social issues of life in South Africa, but the broadcast media made frequent mention of the excellent facilities and organization.

However, there were some implicit examples of the negative portrayal of Africa in live commentaries. To offer one example of this, the USA–Ghana game on 26 June was held at the stadium in Rustenburg. The Radio 5 Live commentary team made frequent reference to smoke blowing into the stadium from surrounding fields, for example: 'A very smoky atmosphere with all the local farmers burning off their crops for the winter', alongside similar phrases relating to the rural nature of the location throughout the elaborative utterances. This situates the stadium at some remove from the urban centres of most European grounds, creating a profound sense of otherness. However, television coverage on ITV2 made no mention of a 'smoke-filled stadium' or of the rural location: in fact, television pictures showed no trace of any hazy atmosphere during the game. This discrepancy between visual image and audio commentary could be explained by an over-enthusiastic commentator attempting to add 'colour' to the local scene, but doing so in a way that reproduces a set of cultural assumptions on the environment and culture of Africa as 'other' and elsewhere.

Conclusion

In this chapter, we have explored some of the linguistic skills and expressive potentials of sports journalism. But we have also highlighted some of the things we might look for in a critical appraisal of the language of sports commentary and coverage. We have seen that the sense of liveness is an important part of sports commentary, but have comprehended that every bit as important is the sense of community, expressed both through the collaboration between the commentators and by means of the assumption of a shared sense of national identity and, occasionally, a sense of injustice. We have also looked at how this sense of national identity is a feature of sports reporting in the print media; how historical tropes and symbols associated with national belonging have become part of the coinage of popular journalism in expressing a national sense of togetherness and its association with the competitiveness of sport; and have seen something of how this attitude can draw upon broader and more invidious cultural assumptions.

6

Online and citizen journalism

Introduction

This chapter will examine what is commonly held to be the main threat to the sanctity of journalism as we have come to know it: the shift online. As we will see, unlike broadcast or print, access to the platforms of delivery is comparatively open, and is as available to 'ordinary' citizens as to professional journalists. This is not to say that media institutions have no proper place or carry no advantage in the online environment. Far from it indeed, and Natalie Fenton (2012: 558) charts the enthusiastic uptake of online technologies by established news corporations, coupled with an emerging 'mutuality and interdependence' of content between online and offline media platforms. The advantages are obvious, and one of the things that Fenton goes on to discuss is how online and digital systems offer capacity and scope that has been difficult to attain in print or conventional broadcast media. Yet, we will see here that online journalism also lends itself to particular forms of engagement that can be understood in terms of the language used, and one of the things we will have established by the end of the chapter is that much online journalism is geared towards contingency of information, along with appropriate forms of authorship.

A threat to journalism?

A great deal of the discussion concerning the shift to online provision that goes on within the journalism profession concerns the impact on those financial models that have sustained the industry for much of the last two centuries. Many of the misgivings stem from World Wide Web–inventor Tim Berners-Lee's vision of the internet as a means of providing and exchanging information in as free a manner as possible. For Berners-Lee (2000: 77), the role of the internet extends beyond the quantity and pliability of the data it is able to store, and is only fully realized when users are able to edit, manipulate and add to the material they find. While this as a vision has only been partially realized – and Wikipedia is a well-known example of its partial enactment – it is the internet that has certainly allowed us to take for granted immediate access to new information, and to assume easy access to the means to distribute information.

But what happens when we turn this towards the distribution of news? We want to highlight three challenges to the conventions of journalism. First is the deprofessionalization of news provision. We will discuss this as we turn towards 'citizen journalism' later in the chapter. Second is the ease of access to news from an ever-greater variety of sources. As the means to produce web content is distributed more widely, professional news producers are encouraged to ensure that the content they produce is used more often and maintains an elevated status. Third, there are technical and informational challenges of the online environment, such that journalism has to adapt to deal with the immediacy and multi-modality of the online world. As Michael Bromley (2010: 31) notes, the age of mass media has tended to move in the direction of 24/7 provision. While Bromley's tone is pessimistic, this does present a significantly greater capacity, offering journalists limitless amounts of space to fill with copy. Journalism also has increasing opportunities for emphasizing the sense of immediacy in a story; updates no longer have to wait until the next scheduled bulletin or paper edition, and rather can be added to a news website on a minute-by-minute basis.

Truth be said, much more than the environment it is instrumental in shaping, the journalism industry has been called upon to meet the challenge of a medium in which information, news and entertainment – the commodities in which journalism trades – have become freely available and subject to more rapid development. The aim here is to offer some ways to understand how the language of journalism is adapting to meet the various challenges presented.

News and contingency: Writing unfolding events

The advantages of online news are particularly pronounced in the reporting of an unfolding story. Even where the details of a story emerge over a period of time, online news is peculiarly able to amend and update content. This can be made particularly complicated when rumours are placed in circulation, and competing accounts and interpretations released by interested groups. The case study that follows in Figure 6.1 provides an example of this;

beginning with an update published on the BBC website, reporting on the fighting in Tripoli during the downfall of Colonel Gadaffi in 2011. The report was composed and posted at a stage in events when the eventual outcome was still comparatively unknown, and Gadaffi himself was still in a position of government:

[Title] Defiant Gadaffi 'vows to fight'	1
Col Muammar Gaddafi has made a speech vowing death or victory in the fight	2
against 'aggression', after Libyan rebels seized his Tripoli compound.	3
In the audio speech, the colonel, whose whereabouts remain unknown, said he	4
had made a 'tactical' retreat from his Bab al-Aziziya compound in the capital.	5
But nobody really believes the claim, a BBC correspondent in Tripoli says.	6
The compound fell on Tuesday to the rebels, who set about demolishing	7
symbols of Col Gaddafi's rule.	8
There were pro-rebel celebrations on the main squares in Tripoli and Benghazi	9
late into Tuesday night but many people are reluctant to celebrate openly until	10
Col Gaddafi and his sons are captured, the BBC's Wyre Davies reports from the	11
city.	12
Colonel Gaddafi called on supporters to 'rise up' and march towards Tripoli	13
At one stage, our correspondent and others had to flee from the ruins of Bab	14
al-Aziziya when snipers opened fire from within.	15
Wednesday morning saw what appeared to be new Nato air strikes in and	16
around Tripoli, our correspondent adds.	17
Known pockets of resistance in the capital include the Abu Salim and al-Hadba	18
districts, and near the Hotel Rixos, where 35 foreign nationals, most of them	19
journalists, have been confined by pro-Gaddafi forces.	20
Fighting has also been reported in the southern desert city of Sebha which has	21
strong Gaddafi family connections. (BBC, 2011)	22

FIGURE 6.1 *BBC News Website, 24 August 2011.*

The style of this report has much in common with longer-established platforms. For example, in the same way as a conventionally structured news story, the opening sentence summarizes the main thrust of the story: Gadaffi's speech and its context. We will recall from our discussion of the work of Labov and story structure in the newspaper chapter that Allan Bell (1991: 149) calls this the 'abstract' of the story, designed to summarize the content and highlight the main point. Also in common with newspaper text, quotation marks are used strategically. Quotes are used as what Gaye Tuchman (1972: 135) calls a 'signalling device', separating out Gadaffi's accusation of 'aggression' and his claim to a 'tactical' response from the authorial voice of the report in a manner designed to question their legitimacy.

However, this is not the only distancing strategy in play. Where the structure differs from what we would expect of newspaper text is the work the author does to maintain their distance from the scene of the conflict, by attributing the report's insights to a correspondent elsewhere in the BBC. These attributions appear as non-defining clauses at the end of sentences (one example is '. . . a BBC correspondent in Tripoli says' on line 6). As non-defining clauses, their removal would not produce a substantial change in meaning, but these clauses are crucial in emphasizing that preceding claims are institutionally sanctioned and come from the scene of the conflict. When we spoke about magazines in Chapter 3, we referred to this form of attribution as 'subordinating conjunctions'. Also in common with what we found in magazines, we can see that these reports use 'indirect speech', where the source's words are rephrased by the correspondent. An example of this is 'Wednesday morning saw what appeared to be new Nato air strikes in and around Tripoli, our correspondent adds' (lines 16–17). Fairclough (1995a: 81) is suspicious of such indirect speech, noting that 'although it is expected to be accurate about the propositional content of what was said, it is ambivalent about the actual words that are used . . . it may transform and translate them into discourses that fit more easily with the reporter's voice'. However, in this case the correspondent joins in the institutional voice of the BBC, so what is the purpose of emphasizing the status of the correspondent here? One notable benefit is to situate the correspondent quoted at the 'discursive centre' of the event. In stressing the credibility of co-presence – the correspondent and the uncertain events within a shared space – these insights submit of a discourse of personal experience. What it feels like to experience a war zone is also made plain, and the verb 'flee' is used to capture the correspondent's sense of danger and urgency.

Of course, it is also possible to use 'direct speech', as we can see in the following report from the CNN website on the same day. The section of the CNN report, given in Figure 6.2, turns to the perspective of the rebel forces (known as the National Transitional Council or the NTC) fighting Gadaffi (spelled in this report using the variant 'Gadhafi').

This section is drawn from the latter half of the report, which is structured around the voices of those directly involved. Two sources are used to describe the situation in Libya: the information minister for the anti-Gadaffi movement Mahmoud Shammam and 'Tripoli resident Maram Wafa'. Their words are separated by a series of shorter interventions from outside: a NATO official speculating on the likely duration of the conflict ('not over yet, although it's close', line 5), a contrary stance by the Venezuelan president on the legitimacy of the NTC rebellion (lines 11–13) and a promise of 'humanitarian aid' from the South Korean government (lines 14–16). The extract itself comes immediately after the report concedes that a key element of information – the whereabouts of Colonel Gadaffi – has yet to be established. The extract picks up where the report interprets Shammam as maintaining that the location of Gadaffi

Mahmoud Shammam, the information minister for the rebel government,	1
the National Transitional Council, said it didn't matter where Gadhafi was.	2
'In a few hours, maximum a few days, we have a new Libya, a new,	3
liberated Libya,' he said Tuesday.	4
A senior NATO official said the war was 'not over yet, although it's close.	5
We continue to watch for flare-ups from around the country, where there	6
are still going to be pockets of resistance. We are also watching the	7
chemical weapons and Scud missiles to make sure they are not used in the	8
endgame.'	9
A growing number of foreign countries are recognizing the rebels' National	10
Transitional Council as Libya's rightful government. But Venezuelan President	11
Hugo Chavez said his country would only recognize a Libyan regime led by	12
Gadhafi, his close ally.	13
On Wednesday, South Korea said the NTC is 'the legitimate governing	14
authority representing the Libyan people.' The South Korean government	15
said it plans to deliver humanitarian aid worth $1 million.	16
Shammam said the release of money that has been frozen in international	17
banks will be critical to the rebels' ultimate success. 'We need to provide	18
ourselves with a lot of necessities and we cannot do this without money,' he	19
said.	20
'Please, please, please, let the international community know – we are	21
hungry for freedom, we are hungry for democracy, we are hungry for a state	22
of law and order and we would like everybody, everybody everywhere in	23
Arab countries and in the international community to support us and help us	24
to get that.'	25
Many Libyan residents who have spoken to CNN did not want to be publicly	26
identified for fear of their safety.	27
But Tripoli resident Maram Wafa, 26, told CNN she wanted to be named	28
because she wants the world to know how proud she is to be a Libyan now.	29
'I see all of the rebels are (about) my age,' Wafa said. 'And at the end, being	30
victorious against the man who has been ruling a country for 42 years – 42	31
years with this iron fist – how can you not be proud?' (CNN, 2011)	32

FIGURE 6.2 *BBC News Website, 24 August 2011.*

had become immaterial, insisting instead that the Libya in prospect is the more important matter. Two direct quotes from Shammam follow. The first of these (beginning 'in a few hours, maximum a few days', line 3) offers some speculation on how quickly the conflict will be resolved, while the second (beginning 'please, please, please, let the international community know', line 21) presents what Scannell (1991) describes as a 'doubly-articulated' address towards the likely CNN audience. So why might direct rather than indirect speech be used here? Both of these quotes have the qualities we would expect of accurately transcribed spontaneous speech, in that they include redundancy and repetition. Yet, in both the repetition performs a rhetorical function, 'few' adding to the sense of imminence and the repeated 'please' conveying the necessary urgency. The same may be said of the quote from resident Maram Wafa, in which the significance of Gadaffi's overthrow is expressed through her rhetorical question ('how can you not be proud?' line 32) and the repetition of '42 years' ('been ruling a country for 42 years – 42 years with this iron fist', lines 31–32). Of course, we need to acknowledge that in order to be incorporated into the story, these words have to be uttered in the first place – but the choice of which quotes to include and the extent to which these are edited invariably invites analysis. Such that this is a stage in the development of the story where a limited amount of concrete information is available, the report focuses more on capturing the emotions and commitment of those involved, drawing upon what Allan Bell (1991: 155) describes as 'the flavour of the eyewitness and colour of direct involvement'.

Of course, what characterizes the online report is the relative lack of restriction on space, and if we look at the beginning of the CNN story (see Figure 6.3) we can detect many of the qualities of the BBC report.

Perhaps the most apparent characteristic about this opening passage is the emotiveness of the language. We can see this is the selection of quotes using direct speech: 'eliminate the criminals, traitors and rats', the metaphor in 'volcano or lava and fire under the feet of the invaders') as well in the main

[Title] Despite seize of Gadhafi complex, regime says it can fight for years	1
Tripoli, Libya (CNN) – Claiming rebels controlled 90% of the country and were	2
days away from 'a new Libya,' the rebel government said it is planning to move	3
many of its key ministries to the Libyan capital of Tripoli on Wednesday.	4
But Libyan ruler Moammar Gadhafi's regime slammed the notion that the battle was	5
over.	6
Two Arabic networks aired an audio message purportedly from Gadhafi that called	7
upon all Libyans 'to clear the city of Tripoli and eliminate the criminals, traitors and	8
rats.'	9
'They are hiding between the families and inside the civilian houses,' the message	10
said. 'It's your duty to enter these houses and take them out.'	11
CNN cannot confirm the authenticity of the message.	12
Hours earlier, Gadhafi spokesman Musa Ibrahim struck an equally defiant tone when	13
he said government forces have the power to fight in Tripoli 'not just for months –	14
for years.'	15
'We will turn Libya into a volcano of lava and fire under the feet of the invaders and	16
their treacherous agents,' Ibrahim said in a phone call to satellite news channels,	17
according to Reuters.	18

FIGURE 6.3 *CNN Website, 25 August 2011.*

text of the report, such as in the used of 'slammed' to describe the incumbent regime's response to reports that their hold is loosening. For all the flourishes of emotion, the report is still careful to emphasize that matters are unfolding and the interpretation of the story might change. Accordingly, there is a modal verb ('claiming', line 2) and adverb ('purportedly', line 7) designed to express an appropriate mood of uncertainty, both in the direction the events are taking and in the veracity of the information CNN has been able to gather. In keeping with this mood of contingency, CNN also include an institutional disclaimer on the veracity of the Gadaffi statement, warning that 'CNN cannot confirm the authenticity of the message'.

Live news writing

It is clear, then, that when online news makes full use of its capacity to deliver instant news while upholding the established conventions of journalism practice, there is the need to balance the emotive potential of a story with the contingency often inherent in an unfolding event. News and the expression of the experience and perception of time are inextricably linked: the very definition of news situates it with the current rather than bygone, the novel over the familiar (Bell, 1995). It seems perfectly natural, then, that news websites such as BBC and CNN emphasize the speed of news delivery and work at providing updates and offering interpretations as they become available. Examples of how this works in practice are to be found in the updatable weblogs available on the news sites of the BBC and other major news organizations. CNN, for example, complement their 'full story' piece (such as the one we look at above) with an updatable blog stream headed 'this just in'.

Figures 6.4 and 6.5 are two extracts from a running blog on the CNN website. Labelled 'latest developments', the first extract shares many of the characteristics of a conventional news story, in giving emphasis to the salient details, and extensive use of sources surrounded with description and contextualization.

It is immediately apparent how an assumption of conditionality is integral to the treatment of sources, even at this stage. News of all the key developments is attributed to a source, usually using direct quotation, and even the acknowledgement of news agency Reuters is contained within a non-defining clause ('according to Reuters', Figure 6.3, line 18). Another feature that predominates is the combination of tenses. As a whole, the text is comparatively free of the conceit of an assumed temporal correspondence of event scripting and reading that often characterizes news texts and their drive for immediacy (see Bell, 1995). Past tense is used to refer to sources

[Updated 7:26 p.m. ET, 1:26 a.m. Wednesday in Libya] Some of the rebel	1
leadership is moving from its power base in Benghazi to the nation's capital, Tripoli,	2
said Mahmoud Shammam, information minister of the rebels' National Transitional	3
Council.	4
'Half of the government will be in Tripoli tomorrow morning,' he said, citing the	5
ministries of Oil, Communications, Interior, Defense and Health. 'They will take care	6
of their jobs immediately.'	7
A stabilization team will ensure that Tripoli is supplied with electricity and clean	8
water, Shammam said.	9
'The whole situation is not so bad,' Shammam told CNN from Libya's border with	10
Tunisia. 'Things are going to get better every day.' But, he added, the work is	11
daunting. Gadhafi left behind no institutions, no political parties, no civil society.	12
'We have to build things from scratch,' he said.	13
	14
[Updated 8:10 p.m. ET, 2:10 a.m. Wednesday in Libya] About 200 people are	15
celebrating in Tripoli's Green Square - which rebels are calling Martyr's Square -	16
CNN's Sara Sidner reports.	17
People are firing guns into the air in celebration, waving pre-Gadhafi Libyan flags	18
and shouting things like 'Gadhafi needs to go,' according to Sidner.	19

FIGURE 6.4 *CNN News Blog, 'This Just In', 20 October 2011.*

[Updated 7:21 p.m. ET, 1:21 a.m. Wednesday in Libya] The information minister	1
of the rebels' National Transitional Council, Mahmoud Shammam, said 'it doesn't	2
matter' where Gadhafi is. [. . .]	3
He said rebel forces controlled 90% of the country. 'In a few hours, maximum a	4
few days, we have a new Libya, a new, liberated Libya,' he said.	5
Shammam said battles raged in several cities across the country - not just in	6
Tripoli. 'We're fighting in three or four fronts right now,' he said, adding, 'our troops	7
are limited.'	8
government forces, civilians have also been wounded, 'which is quite a concern	9
for us,' said Robin W	10
[Updated 8:44 p.m. ET, 2:44 a.m. Wednesday in Libya] Gadhafi, in a taped	11
message aired tonight by a Tripoli radio station, vowed martyrdom or victory,	12
according to Reuters.	13
He also said the retreat from his compound, which was taken over by rebels on	14
Tuesday, was a tactical move, according to Reuters (CNN, 2010).	15
	16
[Updated 9:03 p.m. ET, 3:03 a.m. Wednesday in Libya] A Maltese government	17
spokesman told CNN's Matthew Chance that a boat from Malta has docked in	18
a Libyan port, with space aboard for journalists who are inside the Rixos Hotel	19
in Tripoli. 'The trouble is that we've not managed to negotiate an exit from the	20
hotel,' Chance said early Wednesday. Gadhafi loyalist guards at the hotel have not	21
allowed journalists there to leave, saying they are being protected.	22
	23

FIGURE 6.5 *Continued*

[Updated 9:08 p.m. ET, 3:08 a.m. Wednesday in Libya] Gadhafi spokesman	24
Moussa Ibrahim has told Arrai Television that Libya's tribes have organized a	25
military leadership, and that the tribes will go to Tripoli to fight the rebels.	26
'Moammar Gadhafi's rule is not just over Tripoli,' Ibrahim said. 'Moammar is loved	27
by millions! From the center of Libya to western Libya to the mountains of Libya	28
to everywhere. So the fighting will continue.'	29
	30
[Updated 9:19 p.m. ET, 3:19 a.m. Wednesday in Libya] Rebels at Tripoli's airport	31
say Gadhafi loyalists fiercely defended an area east of the airport Tuesday,	32
prompting the rebels to wonder whether loyalists were protecting a high-profile	33
figure in the vicinity, CNN's Arwa Damon reports.	34
Rebels hold the airport but have yet to control an area to the east. Gadhafi loyalists	35
from two military compounds launched multiple assaults on the airport Tuesday,	36
Damon reported.	37
	38
[Updated 10:58 p.m. ET, 4:58 a.m. Wednesday in Libya] In an interview with	39
CNN, former Gadhafi aide Bashir Saleh called for an end to the violence. 'I appeal	40
to everybody who has his arms to think before shooting - from our side or from the	41
Gadhafi side. It's time to stop the bloodshed,' he said.	42
Asked what Gadhafi had told him during the uprising when he made similar	43
comments, Saleh said, 'He say that he has a job and we have to continue our job.	44
Job is to stop the rebellions, and we have the right to do so.'	45
	46
[Updated 11:11 p.m. ET, 5:11 a.m. Wednesday in Libya] A woman living in Tripoli	47
tells CNN's Anderson Cooper about her neighborhood getting hit by rockets from	48
what she believes were pro-Gadhafi forces, and about how she is proud of the	49
rebels who have risen against Gadhafi [. . .]	50
	51
[Updated 3.37 a.m. ET 9.37 a.m. Wednesday in Libya] CNN's Matthew Chance	52
says pro-Gadhafi guards who have been in the Rixos hotel's lobby armed with	53
assault rifles have largely disappeared from the lobby. But he said international	54
journalists are still not able to leave the hotel. [. . .]	55
Rebels fully controlled the airport but were struggling to control an area east of	56
it early Wednesday. The unexpected resistance caused them to speculate that	57
loyalists could be protecting a high-profile figure in the vicinity (CNN. 2010).	58

FIGURE 6.5 *CNN News Blog, 'This Just In', 20 October 2011.*

either providing information or responding to events ('"In a few hours . . ." he said', 'The information minister . . . said "it doesn't matter"'). Continuing processes and speculation on what may unfold over the coming days are rendered in present and future tense respectively ('Some of the rebel leadership is moving from its power base', 'A stabilization team will ensure that Tripoli is supplied').

Also, in spite of their situation in the temporal order in which they were posted, the entries do not add up to a narrative of the events. In many ways this should come as no surprise, since the expression of news as a 'story' (Fairclough, 1995b: 91) is an arbitrary but vital skill of journalism practice, and certainly does not occur by chance (Bell, 1991). Further distant from these styles of delivery and a narrativized form of journalism, the extract in Figure 6.5 shows how when rendered as a blog, posts are superseded by subsequent entries, and occasional redundancy.

One example of entries being superseded by subsequent posts is the suspected detention of journalists in their hotel. Details of how the journalists are detained in the hotel under armed guard is both posted and marked as 'early Wednesday' (line 21), before an update later says that they are still confined to the premises although 'pro-Gadhafi guards who had been the Rixos hotel's lobby armed with assault rifles have largely disappeared from the lobby' (lines 53–54). There is also the possibility of repetition and redundancy. One report concedes rebel control of the airport, but notes that the area to the east remains contested ('Rebels hold the airport but have yet to control an area to the east', line 35), a situation which is then confirmed in a slightly elaborated version ('Rebels fully controlled the airport but were struggling to control an area east of it', line 56). However, it is expressing the perspectives of the opposing sides as the battles progress that the form of the blog excels. In just this brief extract, and using a combination of direct and reported speech, an NTC spokesman dismisses Gadaffi's whereabouts as irrelevant (lines 2–3); Gadaffi releases a message of 'martyrdom or victory' (line 12); the Maltese government intervenes on behalf of journalists (line 17); a Gadaffi spokesman claims that pro-Gadaffi forces are marshalling throughout Libya (line 24); a former Gadaffi aide calls for an end to the bloodshed (line 42); and a resident of Tripoli describes the city's rocket attacks and her support for the rebel forces (line 47).

In terms of the phenomenology of how the tense can be read, the sense of 'present' within the text is anchored in the moment of writing rather than reading. Tense is used strategically to emphasize the series of shifting and contradictory experiences that lie behind the composition of the story, by showcasing the discursive processes of production. Reading this blog requires submission to what Hemmingway and van Loon (2011) describe as a 'fluid temporal zone', designed to call attention to the experientiality and spontaneity inherent in the assemblage of an online news feed. Yet, in presenting the unfolding events as a series of interpretive moments, coherence gives way to some sense of the confusion, changeability and dynamism of the conflict.

Importantly, for all the 'liveness' of the content, online administrators at the news organization hosting the website have editorial right over the uploading and updating of content. On this basis alone, it is all the more compelling that the contingency, erroneous speculation and repetition is left in place as part of the 'texture' of the online news site. It should be noted that the content of feeds such as this one is often edited and incorporated into reports. The fuller version of this feed, for example, provided the original version of the quote from before referring to 'criminals, traitors and rats', along with the institutional disclaimer as to the line's authenticity. In this way, the blog offers an informational resource for more conventional forms of report. In a discussion of 24-hour broadcast news, Hemmingway and van Loon (2011: 159) describe how this need for scriptedness often means editing the news as the details arrive, as though for the next day's broadcast audience. What sets online journalism apart is the capacity to celebrate unedited copy; to call attention to the volatility of emergent information. Indeed, what such journalism shows is the confusion and conflict involved in newsgathering itself: the reader is invited to behold and even participate in the processes of sense-making.

Online news: The controlling power of the image, and those who control them

This section will go on to discuss how the online environment enables non-professional journalists to contribute to a story as it unfolds, so that they are active agents in the struggle over meaning and truth. In the online environment as elsewhere, the news tends to centre on people: from human interest, through personal tragedy, to demonization and retribution. The climactic moment of the conflict in Libya was to be the capture and subsequent death of Colonel Gadaffi. In common with the conflict that led up to it, information on what fate had befallen Gadaffi emerged in a fractured and contradictory manner. Even while Stephanie Marriott (2007) offers a convincing account of the occasional coverage of unfolding events on other media such as television, we have looked above at how online news is better able to deal with the chronological unfolding of not only the events that make up a news story, but also how the initial ambivalences that often accompany emerging stories can be most accurately represented. It should come as no surprise, then, that online news provision gives the best insight into the reporting of Gadaffi's death, and we will use the example of how the story came to be dealt with on the BBC Online news, and the role of non-professionals in setting the direction of the story, particularly through the use of images mediated through social media.

On 20 October 2011, claims and counter-claims came to be issued about the fate and whereabouts of Gadaffi, and these found expression in the

BBC Online updated news feed (BBC, 2011). At 12.31 British-time, the BBC reported: 'Rumours are reaching us that Col Muammar Gadaffi has been captured and is wounded. A senior NTC figure told Reuters news agency the ex-Libyan leader had been trying to flee Sirte.' The lexical choice here is significant. In opting for the more conjectural 'rumours' over the conventional choice of 'reports', the NTC are positioned as a potentially unreliable source. Where the emerging information is expressed in the more emphatic terms of a 'report', as with the 12.48 update (that 'Anti-Gadaffi radio Voice of Free Libya (VOFL) – based in Benghazi – has reported the arrest. 'The confirmed news is that he has been arrested but it is unknown in which condition,' the station said'), it appears as a technical description of the delivery of news from a media organization, and, in common with the section above, a conditional clause attributing the claim outside of the BBC is included. These initial reports were wise to express caution: an update logged at 12.57 and attributed to pro-NTC media communicates what turned out to be erroneous information that 'Col Gadaffi's son, Mutassim, and former interior minister Abdullah al-Senussi were captured with Col Gadaffi'.

In keeping with the capacity of online news to provide multimedia content, the illustration of the story underwent a similar developmental process. The initial still image used by the BBC to accompany the rumours that Gadaffi had been captured or killed was a shot of triumphal rebels, captioned 'Reports of Col Gadaffi's capture have been greeted with celebrations in Libya'. After several more of celebrating NTC supporters, images more tangibly connected with the capture itself were located and posted. The first of these was taken where Gadaffi was apprehended (posted at approximately 14.31 with the caption 'Here, a NTC fighter looks through a large concrete pipe where Col Gadaffi was allegedly captured, according to reports from the AFP news agency'). The second (see Figure 6.6), and perhaps more resonant image,

FIGURE 6.6 *A gold-plated gun, said to have been owned by the former Libyan leader, has been brandished by those who say he has been captured (BBC News, 2011: 14.48).*

was posted at approximately 14:48, and shows two NTC fighters, including the one said to have made the capture, holding up Gadaffi's gold pistol.

The extent of the conditionality in this caption remains striking. The gun is 'said to have been owned' by Gadaffi, the veracity of whose capture is left to the voice of the fighters rendered in indirect speech ('those who say he has been captured'). However, Figure 6.7 was to offer more visceral evidence of Gadaffi's apprehension, and was taken from a broadcast on Arab news channel Al-Jazeera.

While we have already agreed that the modality of the verb 'purporting' is in keeping with the prevailing mood of caution, the potential existence of a video showing Gadaffi's capture had already been trailed on the news feed in the 14.29 post claiming that Al-Jazeera correspondent Tony Birtley had said on the social media website Twitter that mobile phone footage had become available. After the video of what appears to be a badly injured Gadaffi is broadcast on Al-Jazeera and an image-grab posted on the BBC, the tenor of the BBC feed becomes more emphatic with a corresponding change in the framing of sources. An initial confirmation of the former leader's death is attributed to the news agency Associated Press, and then at approximately 14.48, the BBC post 'Breaking News Libyan Prime Minister Mahmoud Jibril has told a news conference Col Gadaffi is dead, it is confirmed'. At the point of 'it is confirmed', the conjecture and hearsay from earlier in the reports becomes an institutionally sanctioned statement of events, and the British prime minister issues his own statement on Gadaffi's death some minutes later at 15.56.

In assessing which aspects of the reporting of Gadaffi's death were the most important, it is difficult to deny that the videos of his final moments

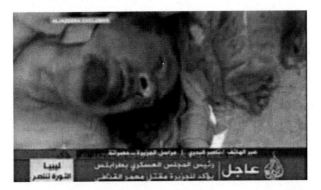

FIGURE 6.7 *Here's a grab of that image from Al-Jazeera purporting to show Col. Gadaffi's body being dragged along the street (BBC News, 2011: 14.59).*

from the NTC fighters and bystanders were to carry the greatest resonance. Certainly, pictures from the scene, and Gadaffi's words in the video, dominated subsequent coverage on television and in newspapers. The still used by the BBC proved to be from one of four videos taken by non-journalists at the scene and edited and unedited extracts were rapidly posted on news sites, online video sites such as MyPlace and links posted to social media sites including Facebook and Twitter. Altogether, the use of mobile technology to record the scene, coupled with news and social media websites to make it available, established the circumstances and meaning of Gadaffi's end in the public imagination.

Citizen input and the struggle for meaning

Control over what is allowed to be represented and how is a crucial component of professional ethics. When another former dictator demonized by the West, Saddam Hussein, was captured by US troops in December 2003, the images released to the media featured the former Iraqi leader undergoing a medical examination. In assessing the conduct of the medical personnel involved, Ian Roberts (2004) used the *British Medical Journal* to suggest that the doctors had neglected their duty to intervene and forbid the filming, in order to protect their patient from public humiliation.

In their selection and presentation, images form part of the language through which the full scope of a news story is relayed. Indeed, as proved to be the case with the death images of both Hussein and Gadaffi, the visual illustration of an event can determine the direction the story will take. However, even while this chapter has emphasized the role of technological affordances, the role of institutions remains an important factor. A prominent example of this is the May 2011 death of Al-Qaida leader Osama bin Laden. Although the shooting was filmed by the US personnel involved, and some in the US government argued for their release, the US executive has until now succeeded in withholding the images from wider release. On this basis, while the film of Saddam's medical examination might have betrayed bad judgement on the part of the professionals involved – certainly the doctors and the American authorities, if not the news media – the images of the deaths of Saddam and Gadaffi illustrate the importance of understanding what happens when the communication of a news event is driven by the interventions of non-journalists. With this in mind, the remainder of this chapter will say more about the characteristics of non-professional input in journalism, and how we might understand the operation of this in an online environment.

Citizen journalism: Practices and identities

We began the chapter by noting that a benefit of online is the potentially limitless amount of space. For news organizations, this is at once an advantage and a disadvantage. On the one hand, any quantity of stories, any amount of explanatory information can be provided through links to online videos, podcasts and pages of text. On the other hand, with this extra capacity comes the expectation and responsibility to provide more material than before. Thurman (2008) looks at the shift towards drawing upon user-generated content. Often, this involves users being invited to submit material to supplement or illustrate the story. During the fighting in Tripoli, for example, the BBC website included at the foot of their pages the message: 'Are you in any of the areas affected by the fighting? Send us your comments and experiences using the form below.' However, the use of citizen-generated content extends beyond the occasional contribution from a normally acquiescent individual, and some way outside of the control of traditional news institutions.

Citizen journalists are those who seek to intervene as journalists, but from outside of a professional/institutional context. Mark Glaser (2012: 478) defines the citizen journalist as someone who 'without journalism training can use the tools of modern technology and the global distribution of the Internet to create, augment or fact-check media on their own or in collaboration with others'. Yet, Glaser acknowledges some considerable overlap between citizen and mainstream, professional journalists. For example, using blogs and other social media, professional journalists can temporarily occupy those realms that have come to be associated with citizen journalism, occasionally engaging the audience in a slightly different tone and marking their input as more 'personal' (commonly, their signature lines include a disclaimer that their views are their own, and not their employers'). Accordingly, broadcast, newspaper and sports journalists in particular are usually encouraged to maintain their own Twitter accounts, wherein their mode of expression falls under the same capacity limits as other users (Hermida, 2010: 299).

Aside from these institutional forays into social media, what purpose does citizen journalism serve? Glaser notes that citizen journalism is driven by the conviction that more knowledge and a greater variety of perspectives are available to the many members of the audience than can be gathered by the institutions of journalism or certainly by the individuals working there. In Fenton's (2012: 559) terms, citizen journalism introduces a greater degree of 'multiplicity and polycentrality' to news, widening the scope of the content beyond that favoured by the established news centres. As well as the introduction of diversity, there is also an increased reach in the collective powers of journalistic surveillance. That is to say, with the exception of a pre-arranged press conference, those positioned around a newsworthy event are more likely to be 'ordinary' citizens going about their daily tasks than professional journalists. Many of these citizens now have the technology to record, email and upload images of what they find, or post unedited accounts of their experiences to a worldwide audience. We saw the entry of non-professional images into the public sphere in the execution of Saddam Hussein, as well as our own example of the capture of Colonel Gadaffi. But what we also saw in both of these cases was the possibility for citizens to record and use images in accordance with their own agenda.

In the analysis of the captioning of these images, as well as the text elaborating on their likely contribution to the news story, we drew attention to the contingency and careful uncertainty of the language. Far from being a limitation on the utility of non-professional images, this is a discourse that contributes to the overall aura of online news: that it is immediate, vital, visceral; with the ever-present danger of undue haste to make public, error and misinterpretation. In keeping with this, those images most attuned to the mood of citizen journalism are those that are explicitly amateurish in their manner. Subject to the sorts of editor restraint described by Thurman (2008: 144), the aura of citizen-input resides in its uncultured, unschooled aura. Low resolution video taken with an unsteady hand, while some way short of professional production standards, are the markers of authenticity in non-professional, citizen-driven content.

In her discussion of new immediacy of journalistic transmission, Angela Phillips (2012) highlights another way in which the inherent immediacy of such citizen journalism environments as social media impacts upon the journalistic mainstream: that of setting the terms of conversation, and subsequent coverage. The # hashtag is a way of flagging the salient word or phrase in a Twitter message. The use of a hashtag attached to a term enables Twitter users to search for a word. As well, when a particular topic is hashtagged by a substantial portion of users within a short period, it is flagged by Twitter as 'trending' and so becomes an item of common currency amongst users. The sudden rise of an item to public prominence in this way falls within the metaphor of 'going viral', and the potential to set the public agenda in this way is as much within the power of charities, NGOs, pressure groups and ordinary citizens as it is with journalists. Twitter therefore distributes the potential for agenda-setting more widely than the traditional journalistic platforms and professional actors.

Online journalism and authorship: Branding

In the chapter on broadcast journalism, we discussed the importance of understanding journalism as a particular form of personalized testimony.

Using the notion that Peters (2001) describes as 'witnessing', it might be helpful for us to think about how useful this might be in understanding the development of online content. In a context in which professional journalists, citizen journalists and interested bystanders jostle on a shared platform, it will be useful to examine the developing language of authorship and identity. Saska Saarkoski (2012) suggests a campaign of 'branding' individuals as reputable authorities: various sorts of agents all perceived as 'valued content producers' (Saarkoski, 2012: 4) with varying qualities of experience, sincerity, expertise, pithiness of expression, professionalism and institutional support. The journalist as 'brand' promises to be a dynamic process: negotiating a cultural antipathy towards 'celebrity journalists' (Saarkoski, 2012: 48) against the professional imperative to gather reputational capital and make content stand out.

In keeping with suggestions of branding, and whether they develop deliberately or implicitly, the popularization of blogs and sites such as Twitter is consistent with a continuing authorial regime in news and comment. Mary Angela Block (2012) argues, as she shows how citizen journalists work at lending 'authority' to their content, this applies as much to individuals as to news corporations. Individuals in a position to tweet from news hot spots can accumulate an archive of work and establish some measure of truth-telling status. The opportunity to use media platforms to bear a particular kind of witness to an event is now as widespread as digital camera or mobile phone ownership allows. As Stuart Allan (2010: 219) points out, many of the most significant examples of citizen journalism do not come from those setting out to establish a reputation. Usually, the most compelling examples come from those 'in the wrong place at the wrong time' and able to report authoritatively on a scenario they happen to inhabit. How, then, are these developments likely to become apparent at the level of representation? A multi-modal approach to online journalism demands attention to the visual and linguistic strategies used to anchor the brand of the individual source, author, journalist or news organization. In other words, we should look at the means and strategies deployed by authors of whatever type to emphasize their particular credentials and warrant to speak.

Across the range of professional and non-professional participants we have examined above, it is therefore worthwhile exploring citizen journalism as a particular form of activity that places an emphasis on certain types of linguistic engagement. This has the advantage of offering some respite from the debate over whether citizen 'journalism' amounts to an abuse of a pseudo-professionalized designation (Glaser, 2012: 581). There may be scope for looking at citizen journalism as a means of providing statement and comment, but without laying claim to professional insight, or the obligations of the trained and accredited news provider. As a form of practice that can be available to professional journalists, given the appropriate symbolic concessions, citizen journalism thus emerges as the performance of a relatively unconstrained form of discursive power, with less emphasis on the practices of objectivity, detachment and balance.

Conclusion

Online journalism is characterized by the rapidity of technological change. It is also apparent that the development of capacity and access to the means of news production are the cause of change within journalism culture itself. There are ever-greater opportunities for a more immediate relationship with unfolding events, which in turn requires a more complex and nuanced relationship with the 'truth' of interpretation. Importantly, the discourses that emerge need to remains true to those commitments to accuracy that should drive journalism of every form and on each media platform. Added to and integrated with this, we have seen the introduction of a raft of non-professional actors into journalism, both in the form of 'citizen journalists' and the participants and bystanders that gather around a news event.

So where should our emphasis lie in analysing online journalism? Such an analysis needs to set apart what distinguishes online journalism from other forms, while appreciating where older discursive conventions remain in place. In this chapter, we have seen that many online news stories share the expressive and structural qualities of longer-established news platforms. But we have also explored the capacity of online news not only to update the news on continually, but to do this cumulatively: that is, to display those updates as a progress towards journalistic understanding. The shifting relationship with the here-and-now of the news text has implications for the experience of reading the news. More importantly, for our purposes, the strategic use of tense, the ambivalence of unverified sourcing and the submission to a default tone of contingency have ongoing implications for the way in which journalism is expressed.

Bibliography

Abu-Lughod, Lila (1990) 'The romance of resistance: Tracing transformations of power through Bedouin women's lives', *American Ethnologist*, 17: 41–55.

Allan, Stuart (2010) *News Culture* (3rd edition). Maidenhead: Open University Press.

Anderson, Benedict (2006) *Imagined Communities* (new edition). London: Verso.

Bakhtin, M. M. (1986) *Speech Genres and Other Late Essays*. Austin: Texas University Press.

Barthes, Roland (1970) *S/Z*. Paris: Seuil.

Barthes, Roland (1970/1975) *S/Z* (trans R. Miller). London: Cape

BBC News (2011) 'As it happened: Libya's Col Gaddafi killed', www.bbc.co.uk/news/world-africa-15387872.

Beard, Adrian (1998) *The Language of Sport*. London: Routledge

Bell, Allan (1991) *The Language of News Media*. Oxford: Blackwell.

—(1995) 'News time', *Time & Society* 4(3): 305–328.

—(1998) 'The discursive structure of news stories', in Bell and Garrett (eds) *Approaches to Media Discourse*. Oxford: Blackwell.

—(1999) 'News stories as narrative', in Adam Jaworski and Nicholas Coupland (eds) *The Discourse Reader*. London: Routledge.

Bell, Allan and Peter Garrett (eds) (1998) *Approaches to Media Discourse*. Oxford: Blackwell.

Bennett, David (1998) (ed.) *Multicultural States: Rethinking Difference and Identity*. London: Routledge.

Benwell, B (2001) Male gossip and language play in the letters pages of men's lifestyle magazines', *Journal of Popular Culture* 34(4): 19–33.

—(2002) 'Is there anything "new" about these lads? The textual and visual construction of masculinity in men's magazines', in Lia Litosseliti and Jane Sunderland (eds) *Gender Identity and Discourse Analysis*. Amsterdam: John Benjamins.

—(ed.) (2003) *Masculinity and Men's Lifestyle Magazines*. Oxford: Blackwell.

—(2004) 'Ironic discourse: Evasive masculinity in men's lifestyle magazines', *Men and Masculinities* 7(1): 3–21.

—(2005) '"Lucky this is anonymous": Ethnographies of reception in men's magazines: a "textual culture" approach', *Discourse and Society* 16(2): 147–172.

Berners-Lee, Tim (2000) *Weaving the Web*. London: Texere.

Billig, Michael (1995) *Banal Nationalism*. London: Sage.

Bishop, Hywel and Adam Jaworski (2003) '"We beat 'em": Nationalism and the hegemony of homogeneity in the British press reportage of Germany versus England during Euro 2000', *Discourse and Society* 14(3): 234–271.

Blain, Neil and Hugh O'Donnell (1998) 'European sports journalism and its readers during Euro 96: Living without *The Sun*', in M. Roche (ed.) *Sport, Popular Culture and Identity*. Aachen: Meyer and Mayer, pp. 37–56.

Blain, Neil, Raymond Boyle and Hugh O'Donnell (1993) *Mass Media and Sports*. Leicester: Leicester University Press.

Block, Mary Angela (2012) 'Citizen video journalists and authority in narrative: Reviving the role of the witness', *Journalism: Theory, Practice and Criticism* 13(5): 639–653.

Bonner, Frances (2003) *Ordinary Television*. London: Sage.

Bourdieu, Pierre (1991) *Language and Symbolic Power*. Cambridge: Polity.

Bromley, Michael (2010) '"All the world's a stage": 24/7 news, newspapers and the ages of media', in Stephen Cushion and Justin Lewis (eds) *The Rise of 24-Hour News Television*. New York: Peter Lang, pp. 31–49.

Brookes, Rod, Justin Lewis and Karin Wahl-Jorgensen (2004) 'The media representation of public opinion: British television news coverage of the 2001 general election', *Media, Culture & Society* 26(1): 63–80.

Brown, Deirdre and Stephen Levinson (1987) *Politeness: Some Universals in Language Use*. Cambridge: Cambridge University Press.

Brown, R. and A. Gilman (1960) 'The pronouns of power and solidarity', in T. A. Sebeok (ed.) *Style in Language*. Cambridge, MA: MIT Press.

Brunsdon, Charlotte and David Morley (1978) *Everyday Television: 'Nationwide'*. London: BFI.

Cameron, Deborah (1990) *The Feminist Critique of Language*. London: Routledge.

—(2001) Working with Spoken Discourse. London: Sage.

—(ed.) (2006) *The Language and Sexuality Reader*. London: Routledge.

Carter, Ronald, Maggie Bowring, Angela Goddard and Danuta Reah (1997) *Working with Texts*. London: Routledge.

Chouliaraki, Lilie (2012) 'Journalism and the visual politics of war and conflict', in Stuart Allan (ed.) *The Routledge Companion to News and Journalism* (2nd edition). Abingdon: Routledge.

Clayman, Stephen (1988) 'Displaying neutrality in television news interviews'. *Social Problems* 35: 474–492.

—(1992) 'Footing in the achievement of neutrality: The case of news interview discourse', in P. Drew and J. Heritage (eds) *Talk at Work*. Cambridge: Cambridge University Press.

—(2002) 'Tribune of the people: Maintaining the legitimacy of aggressive journalism', *Media, Culture & Society* 24: 197–216.

Coates, Jennifer (1995) 'Language, gender and career', in Sara Mills (ed.) *Language and Gender: Interdisciplinary Perspectives*. London: Longman.

—(1996) *Women Talk: Conversation between Women Friends*. Oxford: Blackwell.

Conboy, Martin (2006) *Tabloid Britain: Constructing a Community through Language*. Abingdon: Routledge.

—(2007) *The Language of the News*. London: Routledge.

Connell, Robert W. (1987) *Gender and Power: Society, the Person and Sexual Politics*. Cambridge: Polity.

Corbett, James (2010) *England Expects: A History of the England Football Team* (revised edition). London: De Coubertin.

Coulthard, M. (1996) 'The official version: Audience manipulation in police records of interviews with suspects', in C. R. Caldas-Coulthard and

M. Coulthard (eds) *Texts and Practices: Readings in Critical Discourse Analysis*. London: Routledge.

CNN (2011) 'Despite seize of Gadhafi complex, regime says it can fight for years'.

Cronin, Mike and David Mayall (eds) (1998) *Sporting Nationalisms: Identity, Ethnicity, Immigration and Assimilation*. London: Frank Cass.

Crystal, David (2010) 'Language developments in British English', in Michael Higgins, Clarissa Smith and John Storey (eds) *The Cambridge Companion to Modern British Culture*. Cambridge: Cambridge University Press.

Culler, Jonathan (1975) *Structuralist Poetics: Structuralism, Linguistics and the Study of Language*. London: Routledge.

Cushion, Stephen and Justin Lewis (eds) (2010) *The Rise of 24-Hour News Television*. New York: Peter Lang.

Davis, Anthony (1995) *Magazine Journalism Today*. Oxford: Focal Press.

Delin, Judy (2000) *The Language of Everyday Life*. London: Sage.

Eagleton, Terry (1991) *Ideology: An Introduction*. London: Verso.

Elster, Jon (1982) 'Belief, bias and ideology', in Martin Hollis and Steven Lukes (eds) *Rationality and Relativism*. Oxford: Basil Blackwell.

Ericson, R., P. Baranek and J. Chan (1987) *Visualising Deviance: A Study of News Organisations*. Milton Keynes: Open University Press.

Evans, Harold (1972) *Newsman's English*. London: Heinemann.

Fairclough, Norman (2001 [1989]) *Language and Power*. Harlow: Longman.

—(1992) *Discourse and Social Change*. London: Sage.

—(1993) 'Critical Discourse Analysis and the marketization of public discourse: The universities', in *Discourse and Society* 2: 133–168.

—(1995a) *Critical Discourse Analysis: The Critical Study of Language*. Harlow: Longman.

—(1995b) *Media Discourse*. London: Arnold.

—(1998) 'Political discourse in the media: An analytical framework', in A. Bell and P. Garret (eds) *Approaches to Media Discourse*. Oxford: Blackwell.

—(2002) 'Critical discourse analysis as a method in social scientific research', in Ruth Wodak and Michael Meyer (eds) *Methods of Critical Discourse Analysis*. London: Sage.

—(2003) *Analysing Discourse: Textual Analysis for Social Research*. London: Routledge.

Fairclough, Norman and Ruth Wodak (1997) 'Critical Discourse Analysis', in T. A. van Dijk (ed.) *Discourse as Social Interaction*. London: Sage.

Fenton, Natalie (2012) 'News in the digital age', in Stuart Allan (ed.) *The Routledge Companion to News and Journalism* (revised edition). Abingdon: Routledge, pp. 557–567.

Foucault, Michel (1981) 'The order of discourse', in R. Young (ed.) *Untying the Text: A Poststructuralist Reader*. Oxford: Basil Blackwell.

Fowler Robert, B. Hodge, G. Kress and T. Trew (1979) *Language and Control*. London: Routledge.

Frow, John (1989) 'Discourse and power', in Mike Gane (ed.) *Ideological Representation and Power in Social Relations*. London. Routledge.

Galtung, Johan and Mari Ruge (1965) 'The structure of foreign news. The presentation of the Congo, Cuba and Cyprus crises in four Norwegian newspapers', *Journal of Peace Research* 2: 64–90.

Garland, J. and M. Rowe (1999) 'Selling the game short: An examination of the role of antiracism in British football', *Sociology of Sport Journal* 16(1): 35–53.

Gauntlett, David (2002) *Media, Gender and Identity*. London: Routledge.

Gee, Paul (1999) *An Introduction to Discourse Analysis: Theory and Method*. London: Routledge.

Gellner, Ernest (1983) *Nations and Nationalism*. Oxford: Blackwell.

Glaser, Mark (2012) 'Citizen journalism: Widening world views, extending democracy', in Stuart Allan (ed.) *The Routledge Companion to News and Journalism* (revised edition). Abingdon: Routledge.

Goddard, Angela (1998) *The Language of Advertising*. London: Routledge.

Goffman, Erving (1959) *The Presentation of Self in Everyday Life*. Harmondsworth: Penguin.

—(1981) *Forms of Talk*. Oxford: Blackwell.

Graddol, David, Jenny Cheshire and Joan Swann (1999 [1994]) *Describing Language*. Buckingham: Open University Press.

Gramsci, Antonio (1971) *Selections from the Prison Notebooks*. London: Lawrence & Wishart.

—(1998) *Prison Letters* (trans. Hamish Henderson). London: Pluto Press.

Grice, H. Paul (1975) 'Logic and conversation' in P. Cole and J. P. Morgan (eds) *Syntax and Semantics 3: Speech Acts*. New York: Academic Press.

Habermas, Jürgen (1987) *Theory of Communicative Action, vol. 1*. London: Heinemann.

Hall, Stuart (1997) 'The question of cultural identity', in S. Hall, D. Held and T. McGrew (eds) *Modernity and Its Futures*. Cambridge: Polity.

—(1992) *Representation: Cultural Representations and Signifying Practices*. London: Sage.

Hall, S., C. Critcher, T. Jefferson, J. Clarke and B. Roberts (1978) *Policing the Crisis: Mugging, the Sae and Law and Order*. London: Macmillan.

Halliday, Michael A. K. (1975) 'Anti-languages', *American Anthropologist* 78(3): 570–584.

Harcup, Tony (2009) *Journalism: Principles and Practice* (2nd edition). London: Sage.

Harcup, Tony and Deirdre O'Neill (2001) 'What is news? Galtung and Ruge revisited', *Journalism Studies* 2(2): 261–280.

Hartley, John (1990) *Understanding News*. London: Methuen.

Hartley, John and Martin Montgomery (1985) 'Representation and relations: Ideology and power in the press and TV news', in T. A. van Dijk (ed.) *Discourse and Communication*. Berlin: Walter de Gruyter.

Helmer, James (1993) 'Storytelling in the creation and maintenance of organizational tension and stratification', *The Southern Communication Journal*, 59: 34–44.

Hemmingway, Emma and Joos van Loon (2011) '"We'll always stay with live until we have something better to go to . . .": the chronograms of 24-hour television news', *Time & Society* 20(2): 149–170.

Hennessey, Brendan (1989) *Writing Feature Articles: A Practical Guide to Methods and Markets*. Oxford: Heinemann.

Heritage, J. (1985) 'Analysing news interviews: Aspects of the production of talk for overhearing audiences', in T. A. van Dijk (ed.) *Handbook of Discourse Analysis, Vol 3: Discourse and Dialogue*. London: Academic Press.

Heritage, J. and D. Greatbatch (1991) 'On the institutional character of institutional overhearing audiences' in T. A. van Dijk (ed.) *Handbook of Discourse Analysis, Vol 3: Discourse and Dialogue*. London: Academic Press.

Hermida, Alfred (2009) 'The blogging BBC', *Journalism Practice* 3(3): 268–284.

—(2010) 'Twittering the news: The emergence of ambient journalism', *Journalism Practice* 4(3): 297–308.

Higgins, Michael (2004) 'Putting the nation in the news', *Discourse & Society* 15(5): 633–648.

—(2006) 'Substantiating a political public sphere in the Scottish press', *Journalism: Theory, Practice and Criticism* 7(1): 25–44.

—(2008) *Media and Their Publics*. Maidenhead: OUP.

—(2010) 'British newspapers today' in M. Higgins, C. Smith and J. Storey (eds). *The Cambridge Companion to Modern British Culture*. Cambridge: Cambridge University Press.

Higgins, Michael and Angela Smith (2011) 'Not one of U.S.: Kate Adie's report of the 1986 US bombing of Tripoli and its critical aftermath', *Journalism Studies* 12(3): 344–358.

—(2013) '"My husband, my hero": Selling the spouses in the 2010 general election', *Journal of Political Marketing 12(2): in press.*

Hobsbawm, E. J. (1990) *Nations and Nationalism since 1780*. Cambridge: Cambridge University Press.

Hobsbawm, E. J. and Ranger T. (eds) (1983) *The Invention of Tradition*. Cambridge: Cambridge University Press.

Hodge, Robert and Gunther Kress (1993 [1979]) *Language as Ideology*. London: Routledge.

Holquist, M. (1981) *Dialogism: Bakhtin and His Works*. London: Routledge.

Horton, D. and R. R. Wohl (1982) 'Mass communication and para-social interaction: Observation of intimacy at a distance', in G. Gumpert and R. Cathcart (eds) *Inter/Media: Interpersonal Communication in a Media World*. New York: Oxford University Press.

Hutchby, Ian (1996) *Confrontation Talk*. Mahwah, NJ: Lawrence Erlbaum Associates.

—(2006) *Media Talk*. Maidenhead: Open University Press.

Jackson, Peter, Nick Stevenson, and Kate Brooks (2001) *Making Sense of Men's Magazines*. Cambridge: Polity.

Jaworski, Adam and Coupland, Nicholas (eds) (1999) *The Discourse Reader*. London: Routledge.

Kress, Gunther (1985) *Linguistic Process in Sociocultural Practice*. Geelong, Victoria: Deakin University Press.

Kress, Gunther and Terry Threadgold (1988) 'Towards a social theory of genre', *Southern Review* 21(3): 215–243.

Labov, William (1972) *Sociolinguistics Patterns*. Philadelphia: University of Pennsylvania Press.

Labov, William and J. Walestsky (1967) 'Narrative analysis: Oral versions of personal experience', in J. Helm (ed.) *Essays on the Verbal and Visual Arts*. Seattle: University of Washington Press.

Lewis, Justin, Terry Threadgold, Rob Brookes and Nick Mosdell (n.d.) 'Too close for comfort? The role of embedded reporting during the 2003 Iraq War: Summary report'. Cardiff: JOMEC.

Love, R. L. (1965) 'The business of television and the Black Weekend', in Bradley S. Greenberg and Edwin B. Parker (eds) *The Kennedy Assassination and the American public*. Stanford, CA: Stanford University Press.

McCombs, Maxwell (2004) *Setting the Agenda: The Mass Media and Public Opinion*. Cambridge: Polity.

McCracken, Ellen (1992) *Decoding Women's Magazines*. Basingstoke: Macmillan.

Macdonald, Myra (1995) *Representing Women: Myths of Femininity in the Popular Media*. London: Arnold.

—(2003) *Exploring Media Discourse*. London: Arnold.

McLoughlin, Linda (2000) *The Language of Magazines*. London: Routledge.

Maguire, Joseph and Jason Tuck (1998) 'Global sports and patriot games: Rugby union and national identity in the United Sporting Kingdom since 1945', in M. Cronin and D. Mayall (eds) *Sporting Nationalisms*. London: Frank Cass.

Maguire, Joseph and Jason Tuck (1998) 'Global sports and patriot games: Rugby union and national identity in the United Sporting Kingdom since 1945', in Mike Cronin and David Mayall (eds) *Sporting Nationalisms: Identity, Ethnicity, Immigration and Assimilation*. London: Frank Cass, pp. 103–126.

Maguire, Joseph, Emma Poulton and Catherine Possamai (1999) 'Weltkrieg III? Media coverage of England versus German in Euro 96', *Journal of Sport and Social Issues* 23(4): 439–454.

Marriott, Stephanie (2007) *Live Television*. London: Sage.

Marshall, Jill and Werndly Angela (2002) *The Language of Television*. London: Routledge.

Matheson, Donald (2005) *Media Discourses: Analysing Media Texts*. Maidenhead: Open University Press.

Miller, C. and K. Swift (1995) *The Handbook of Non-Sexist Writing for Writers*. London: Women's Press.

Montgomery, Martin (1995) *An Introduction to Language and Society*. London: Routledge.

—(2006) 'Broadcast news, the live "two-way" and the case of Andrew Gilligan', *Media, Culture and Society* 28(2): 233–259.

—(2007) *The Discourse of Broadcast News: A Linguistic Approach*. London: Routledge.

Morley, David (1980) *The 'Nationwide' Audience*. London: BFI.

Myers, Greg (1994) *Words in Ads*. London: Arnold.

Nah, Shungahn and Deborah S. Chung (2012) 'When citizens meet both professional and citizen journalists: Social trust, media credibility, and perceived journalistic roles among online community news readers', *Journalism: Theory, Practice and Criticism* 13(6): 714–730.

Ofcom (2011) *The Ofcom Broadcasting Code*. London: Ofcom.

Pearce, Michael (2006) *The Routledge Dictionary of English Language Studies*. London: Routledge.

Peters, John Durham (2001) 'Witnessing', *Media, Culture & Society* 23(6): 707–723.

Phillips, Angela (2012) 'Sociability, speed and quality in the changing news environment', *Journalism Practice* 6(5–6): 669–679.

Quirk, R., S. Greenbaum, G. Leech and K. Svartvik (1985) *A Comprehensive Grammar of the English Language*. London: Longman.

Reah, Danuta (1998) *The Language of Newspapers*. London: Routledge.

Reisigl, Martin and Ruth Wodak (2001) *Discourses of Discrimination: Rhetorics of Racism and Anti-Semitism*. London: Routledge.

Roberts, Ian (2004) 'Saddam Hussein's medical examination should not have been broadcast: Images were designed to humiliate', *British Medical Journal* 328(7430): 51.

Rowe, David (2004) *Sport, Culture and the Media* (2nd edition). Maidenhead: Open University Press.

—(2007) 'Sports journalism: Still the "toy department" of the news media?', *Journalism: Theory, Practice and Criticism* 8(4): 385–405.

Saarkoski, Saska (2012) *Brands, Stars and Regular Hacks*. Oxford: Reuters Institute for the Study of Journalism.

Sacks, Harvey (1992) *Lectures in Conversation*. Oxford: Blackwell.

Scannell, Paddy (ed.) (1991) 'Introduction: The relevance of talk', in Scannell (ed.) *Broadcast Talk*. London: Sage.

—(1996) *Radio, Television and Modern Life*. Oxford: Blackwell.

Schiffrin, Deborah (1984) 'Jewish argument as sociability', *Language in Society* 13: 311–335.

Schudson, M. (1982) 'The ideal of conversation in the study of mass media', in G. Gumpert and R. Cathcart (eds) *Inter/Media: Interpersonal Communication in a Media World*. New York: Oxford University Press.

—(2001) 'The objectivity norm in American journalism', *Journalism* 2(2): 149–170.

Searle, John R. (1969) *Speech Acts: An Essay on the Philosophy of Language*. Cambridge: Cambridge University Press.

Silberstein, Sandra (2002) *War of Words: Language, Politics and 9/11*. London: Routledge.

Simpson, Paul (1993) *Language, Ideology and Point of View*. London: Routledge.

—(1998) *Nationalism and Modernism*. London: Routledge.

Smith, Angela (2009) 'Tabloid television', in C. H. Sterling (ed.) *Encyclopaedia of Journalism* 4: Q-Z. Thousand Oaks, CA: Sage.

Smith, Angela and Michael Higgins (2012) 'The convenient ambiguity of tone', *Journalism: Theory, Practice and Criticism* 13(8): 1081–1095.

Smith, Anthony D. (1991) *National Identity*. Harmondsworth: Penguin.

Spender, D. (1980) *Man Made Language*. London: Routledge.

Sperber, Dan and Deirdre Wilson (1995) *Relevance: Communication and Cognition* (2nd edition). Oxford: Blackwell.

Spiegl, F. (1989) *Mediawrite/mediaspeak*. London: Elm Tree.

Starkey, Guy (2007) *Balance and Bias in Journalism*. London: Routledge.

Storey, John (1997 [1993]) *An Introduction to Cultural Theory and Popular Culture*. Hemel Hempstead: Harvester Wheatsheaf.

Talbot, Mary (1995) 'A synthetic sisterhood: False friends in a teenage magazine', in Hall and Bucholtz (eds) *Gender Articulated: Language and the Socially Constructed Self*. London: Routledge.

—(2010 [1998]) *Language and Gender* (2nd edition). Cambridge: Polity.

Talbot, Mary, Karen Atkinson and David Atkinson (2003) *Language and Power in the Modern World*. Edinburgh University Press.

Tannen, Deborah (1991) *You Just Don't Understand*. London: Virago.

—(1995) *Talking from 9 to 5*. London: Virago.

Temple, Mick (2008) *The British Press*. Maidenhead: Open University Press.

Thibault, P. J. (1991) *Social Semiotics as Praxis: Text, Social Meaning Making, and Nabakov's Ada*. Minneapolis: University of Minneapolis Press.

Thompson, John B. (1995) *The Media and Modernity*. Cambridge: Polity.

Threadgold, Terry (1989) 'Talking about genre: Ideologies and incompatible discourses', *Cultural Studies* 2(1): 101–127.

—(1997) *Feminist Poetics: Poiesis, Performance, Histories*. London: Routledge.

Thurman, Neil (2008) 'Forums for citizen journalists? Adoption of user generated content initiatives by online news media', *New Media and Society* 10(1): 139–157.

—(2011) 'Making "The Daily Me": Technology, economics and habit in the mainstream assimilation of personalized news', *Journalism: Theory, Practice & Criticism* 12(4): 395–415.

Tolson, Andrew (2006) *Media Talk: Spoken Discourse on TV and Radio*. Edinburgh: Edinburgh University Press.

Tuchman, Gaye (1972) 'Objectivity as strategic ritual: An examination of newsmen's notions of objectivity', *American Journal of Sociology* 77(4): 660–679.

Tulloch, John and Colin Sparks (2000) *Tabloid Tales*. London: Rowman and Littlefield.

van Dijk, Teun (1983) *News as Discourse*. Hillsdale, NJ: LEA.

—(1988) *News as Discourse*. Hillsdale, NJ: Lawrence Erlbaum.

—(1991) *Racism and the Press*. London: Routledge.

Varley, N. (1999) 'Away the lads', *The Guardian* 12 April.

Vesanen, Jan (2007) 'What is personalisation? A conceptual framework', *European Journal of Marketing* 41(5/6): 409–418.

Whannel, Garry (1992) *Fields of Vision: Television Sport and Cultural Transformation*. London: Routledge.

Williamson, Judith (1995) *Decoding Advertisements: Ideology and Meaning in Advertising*. London: Marion Boyers.

Wodak, Ruth, P. Nowak, J. Pelikan, H. Gruber, R. de Cillian and R. Mitten (1990) 'Wir sind alle unschuldige Täter', in *Diskurshistorische Studien zum Nachkriegantisemitismus*. Frankfurt: Suhrkamp.

Wodak, Ruth (1996) *Disorders of Discourse*. Harlow: Longman.

—(2002) 'The discourse-historical approach', in Ruth Wodak and Michael Meyer (eds) *Methods of Critical Discourse Analysis*. London: Sage.

Wodak, Ruth and Tuen van Dijk (2000) *Racism at the Top*. Klagenfurt: Drava.

Wodak, Ruth and J. R. Martin (eds) (2003) *Re/reading the Past: Critical and Functional Perspectives on Time and Value*. Amsterdam: John Benjamins.

Wodak, Ruth and Michael Meyer (eds) (2002) *Methods of Critical Discourse Analysis*. London: Sage.

Wodak, Ruth and Michael Meyer (2009) 'Critical discourse analysis: History, agenda, theory and methodology', in *Methods of Critical Discourse Analysis* (2nd edition). London: Sage.

Wodak, Ruth, R. De Cellia, M. Reisigl and K. Liebhart (1999) *The Discursive Construction of National Identity*. Edinburgh: Edinburgh University Press.

Yule, George (1996) *Pragmatics*. Oxford: Oxford University Press.

—(2006) *The Study of Language* (3rd edition). Cambridge: Cambridge University Press.

Index